ROMAN KRZNARIC is an author, cultural think[illegible]ng faculty member of The School of Life [illegible]ches courses about work. He has been na[illegible] one of Britain's leading lifestyle think[illegible]izations including Oxfam and the Unite[illegible] using empathy and conversation to create social change. [illegible] more, see www.romankrznaric.com

THE SCHOOL OF LIFE is dedicated to exploring life's big questions: *How can we fulfil our potential? Can work be inspiring? Why does community matter? Can relationships last a lifetime?* We don't have all the answers, but we will direct you towards a variety of useful ideas – from philosophy to literature, psychology to the visual arts – that are guaranteed to stimulate, provoke, nourish and console.

www.theschooloflife.com

By the same author:

The Wonderbox: Curious Histories of How To Live

The First Beautiful Game: Stories of Obsession in Real Tennis

How to Find Fulfilling Work

Roman Krznaric

MACMILLAN

First published 2012 by Macmillan
an imprint of Pan Macmillan, a division
of Macmillan Publishers Limited

Pan Macmillan
20 New Wharf Road, London N1 9RR
Basingstoke and Oxford
Associated companies throughout the world
www.panmacmillan.com

ISBN 978-1-4472-0228-8

Case studies, except when the author is the subject of them, have been fictionalized and have had names changed to protect the identities of the people concerned.

9

A CIP catalogue record for this book is available from the British Library.

Cover designed by Marcia Mihotich
Text design and setting by seagulls.net
Printed and bound by CPI Group (UK) Ltd, Croydon, CR0 4YY

Contents

The thought once occurred to me that if one wanted to crush and destroy a man entirely, to mete out to him the most terrible punishment, one at which the most fearsome murderer would tremble, shrinking from it in advance, all one would have to do would be to make him do work that was completely and utterly devoid of usefulness and meaning.
– Fyodor Dostoyevsky

1. The Age of Fulfilment

Three Career Tales

Rob Archer grew up on a housing estate in Liverpool where there was 50 per cent unemployment and the main industry was heroin. He fought his way out, studying hard and getting to university, and found a great job as a management consultant in London. He was earning plenty of money, he had interesting clients and his family was proud of him. 'I should have been very happy, but I was utterly miserable,' he recalls. 'I remember being put on assignments in which I had no background but was presented as an expert. I was supposed to know about knowledge management and IT, but it all left me cold, and I always felt like an outsider.' He did his best to ignore his feelings:

> I assumed I should be grateful to just have a job, let alone a 'good' one. So I focused harder on trying to fit in and when that didn't work, I lived for the weekend. I did this for ten years, burning the candle at both ends. Eventually it caught up with me. I became chronically stressed and anxious. Then one day I had to ask the CEO's personal assistant to call me an ambulance because I thought I was having a heart attack. It turned out to be a panic attack. That's when I knew I couldn't go on.

> The problem was that all the alternatives – changing career, starting over again – seemed impossible. How could I trade in the security of my comfortable life for uncertainty? Wouldn't I be risking all the progress I had made? I also felt guilt that I should even be searching for such luxuries as 'meaning' and 'fulfilment'. Would my grandfather have complained at such fortune? Life appeared to offer an awful choice: money or meaning.

At the age of sixteen, Sameera Khan decided that she wanted to become a lawyer. She was driven partly by her interest in human rights and Amnesty International, and partly by the enticing glamour of her favourite TV series, *LA Law*. But she also wanted to do something that would please her parents, Pakistani and East African Indian immigrants, who had arrived in Britain in the 1960s, her dad working his way up from a factory job, and both of them becoming successful social-worker managers. 'For them, success is measured through tangible career rungs in a profession like law, medicine or accountancy,' says Sameera, who is now in her early thirties. 'Their expectations influenced my decision 150 per cent.' She followed her plan, getting a law degree, then spending her twenties qualifying as a solicitor. She found a position as an in-house corporate lawyer for a hedge fund. 'I had it all, I was a City Girl earning megabucks, and loved the way law used my brain.' But after five years in the job, it all suddenly changed:

> I was on honeymoon, sitting on a beach in Sicily, when I had an epiphany. I realized something wasn't right. I'd just got

married, which was a huge rite of passage in my life and I should have been ecstatic. I'd achieved my dream of becoming a lawyer, and I had my partner by my side. Yet I felt totally unfulfilled. Where were the 'my life is now perfect' sparks? And as I sat there I worked out that the problem must be my career. I could see its future so clearly laid out before me and it filled me with dread. I realized that I wasn't going to be happy sitting behind a desk for the next forty years – for the rest of my life – making rich people richer. I had worked really hard to get this qualification in a respected profession, but was now left thinking, 'Surely my career should offer me more than this. Is this it? Is this all I get from life?' When it dawned on me that my career to date felt somewhat meaningless, it was devastating.

I was really scared about contemplating anything but law. Law identified me; indeed, I thought it defined me. A lot of lawyers are like this – it's your label, it's who you are. To lose that identity was going to make me feel naked and completely empty. If you're not a lawyer, what are you? *Who* are you? When I got back from my honeymoon, I could see that I was getting myself into a downward spiral of job-related despair, but I didn't know how to fix it. I literally went to Google and typed in something like 'What to do if you hate your career'.

Iain King has never been conventional. When he left secondary school, he spent a year busking around Europe – playing the guitar standing on his head. One summer while at college in the early 1990s, he and a friend crossed into northern Iraq from Turkey, where they befriended a group of Kurdish freedom fighters, travelled around with them in a Jeep full of machine guns and hand-held missile launchers, and narrowly escaped being kidnapped. Later, Iain started up a national student newspaper, which folded after half a dozen issues, then volunteered as a researcher for a political party. Never having had much of a career plan, he ended up as an expert on peace-building for the United Nations and other international organizations. He helped introduce a new currency in Kosovo and has worked alongside soldiers on the battlefront in Afghanistan. He has also found time to write a philosophy book, and to spend a year as a househusband in Syria, the lone father at baby groups in the Damascus expatriate community.

When Iain's wife was pregnant with their second child, he decided it was time to give up his precarious freelance career and get a steady job back in London to support his family. He found a post in the civil service, and now advises the government on its overseas humanitarian policies. He describes it with great enthusiasm: the issues are fascinating, the people stimulating, and he is using his first-hand knowledge of conflict situations. Yet there is a lurking discomfort. Somehow being a civil servant doesn't quite fit with how he sees himself. Work and self are out of alignment:

> The job is interesting but it's rather conventional for the kind of person I am. I feel it isn't the permanent me. When I sit on the tube in the morning, I sometimes notice that I'm wearing a suit, and I'm forty, I'm middle-class, I'm white, I'm male, and I live in one of the more conventional suburbs of London. And I think, 'Where's the guy who used to stand on his head in the tube and play the guitar?'

> On the face of it I look like a very conventional person, yet I still regard myself as deeply unconventional. Paradox is too strong a word, but there's a tension there. At this time in my life, I have to accept the tension. I'm more conventional than I might otherwise be because I've got young kids and I'm the single breadwinner. I'm not about to leave my job, but I sometimes wonder, 'Should I really stick with this forever?'

Great Expectations

The desire for fulfilling work – a job that provides a deep sense of purpose, and reflects our values, passions and personality – is a modern invention. Open Samuel Johnson's celebrated *Dictionary*, published in 1755, and you will discover that the word 'fulfilment' does not even appear.[1] For centuries, most inhabitants of the Western world were too busy struggling to meet their subsistence needs to worry about whether they had an exciting career that used their talents and nurtured their wellbeing. But today, the spread of material prosperity has freed our minds to expect much more from the adventure of life.

We have entered a new age of fulfilment, in which the great dream is to trade up from money to meaning. For Rob, Sameera and Iain, it is not enough to have a respectable career offering the old-fashioned benefits of a healthy salary and job security. Paying the mortgage still matters, but they need more to feed their existential hungers. And they are not the only ones. In the course of researching this book I spoke to scores of people, from over a dozen countries, about their career journeys. From stressed bankers to tired waitresses, from young graduates burdened by student loans to mothers attempting to return to the paid workforce, almost all of them aspired to have a job that was worth far more than the pay check.

Yet for most of them, the task of finding a fulfilling career was one of the biggest challenges of their lives. Some were stuck in uninspiring jobs they felt unable to escape, trapped by a lack of opportunity or a lack of self-confidence. Others had, after trial and error, eventually found work they loved. Many were still engaged in the search, while there were those who didn't know where to begin. Nearly all had faced moments when they realized that work wasn't working for them, whether the trigger for this was a panic attack, an epiphany, or a creeping recognition that they were on a treadmill that was taking them nowhere. The wisdom in their career-change stories emerges from them not being golden tales full of smooth transitions and happy endings, but rather complex, challenging and often arduous personal struggles.

Their experiences reflect the emergence of two new afflictions in the modern workplace, both unprecedented in history: a plague of job dissatisfaction, and a related epidemic of uncertainty about how to choose the right career. Never have so many people felt so unfulfilled in their career roles, and been so unsure what to do about it. Most surveys in the West reveal that at least half the workforce are unhappy in their jobs. One cross-European study showed that 60 per cent of workers would choose a different career if they could start again. In the United States, job satisfaction is at its lowest level – 45 per cent – since record-keeping began over two decades ago.[2] Added to this is the death of the 'job for life', now a quaint relic of the twentieth century. In its place is a world of short-term contracts, temping, and nomadic career wanderings, where the average job lasts only four years, forcing us to make more and more choices, often against our wishes.[3] Choosing a career is no longer just a decision we make – often frighteningly uninformed – as a spotty teenager or wide-eyed twenty-something. It has become a dilemma we will face repeatedly throughout our working lives.

The yearning for a fulfilling career may have begun to permeate our expectations, but is it really possible to find a job in which we can thrive and feel fully alive? Is it not a utopian ideal reserved for the privileged few who can afford fancy education, who have the financial means to risk opening a baby-yoga cafe, or who have the social connections required to win the coveted prize of a job they love?

There are two broad ways of thinking about these questions. The first is the 'grin and bear it' approach. This is the view that we should get our expectations under control and recognize that work, for the vast majority of humanity – including ourselves – is mostly drudgery and always will be. Forget the heady dream of fulfilment and remember Mark Twain's maxim, 'Work is a necessary evil to be avoided.' From the forced labour used to build the pyramids through to the soulless McJobs of the twenty-first-century service sector, the story of work has been one of hardship and tedium. This history is captured in the word itself. The Russian for work, *robota*, comes from the word for slave, *rab*. The Latin *labor* means drudgery or toil, while the French *travail* derives from the *tripalium*, an ancient Roman instrument of torture made of three sticks.[4] We might therefore adopt the early Christian view that work is a curse, a punishment for the sins of the Garden of Eden, when God condemned us to getting our daily bread by the sweat of our brows. If the Bible isn't to your spiritual taste, try Buddhism, which upholds the belief that all life is suffering. 'Anguish,' writes the Buddhist thinker Stephen Batchelor, 'emerges from craving for life to be other than it is.'[5] The message of the 'grin and bear it' school of thought is that we need to accept the inevitable and put up with whatever job we can get, as long as it meets our financial needs and leaves us enough time to pursue our 'real life' outside office hours. The best way to protect ourselves from all the optimistic pundits pedalling fulfilment is to develop a hardy philosophy of acceptance, even resignation, and not set our hearts on finding a meaningful career.

I am more hopeful than this, and subscribe to a different approach, which is that it is possible to find work that is life-enhancing, that broadens our horizons and makes us feel more human. Although the search for a fulfilling career has only become a widespread aspiration in the West since the end of the Second World War, it has its roots in the rise of individualism in Renaissance Europe. This was the era in which celebrating your uniqueness first became fashionable. The Renaissance is well known for having produced extraordinary advances in the arts and sciences, which helped to shake off the shackles of medieval Church dogma and social conformity. But it also gave birth to highly personalized cultural innovations, such as the self-portrait, the intimate diary, the genre of autobiography and the personal seal on letters. In doing so, it legitimized the idea of shaping your own identity and destiny.[6] We are the inheritors of this tradition of self-expression. Just as we seek to express our individuality in the clothes we wear or the music we listen to, so too we should search for work that enables us to express who we are, and who we want to be.

It is possible to find work that is life-enhancing and broadens our horizons.

Some people, especially those living on the social margins of poverty and discrimination, may have almost no opportunity to achieve this goal. That I recognize. If you are trying to support your family on the minimum wage or are queuing up at the local job centre during an economic downturn, the idea of a life-enhancing career might come across as a luxury.

For the majority living in the affluent West, however, there is nothing utopian about the idea of a fulfilling career. The hardships that existed in the past have eased. You are unlikely to wake up tomorrow with no other option than working a fourteen-hour day in a Lancashire textile mill or to find yourself picking cotton on a slave plantation in Mississippi. As we will discover, the landscape of career choice has opened up remarkably over the past century, offering a new vista of purposeful possibilities. Yes, the bar has been raised: we expect much more from our jobs than previous generations. But when somebody asks us the deadening question 'What do you do?', let us set our sights on giving an enlivening answer, which makes us feel that we are doing something truly worthwhile with our lives, rather than wasting away the years in a career that will leave the bitter taste of regret in our mouths.

Grin and bear it? Forget it. This is a book for those who are looking for a job that is big enough for their spirit, something more than a 'day job' whose main function is to pay the bills. It is a guide for helping you take your working life in new directions, and for bringing your career and who you are into closer alignment.

My approach is to interweave an exploration of two vital questions. First, what are the core elements of a fulfilling career? We need to know what we are actually searching for, and it turns out that there are three essential ingredients: meaning, flow and freedom. None of them are easy to attain, and their pursuit raises inevitable tensions. For instance, should we prefer a career that offers great pay and social status over working for a cause we believe in, with the prospect of making a difference? Should we aspire to be a high achiever in a specialized field, or a 'wide achiever' across several fields? And how can we balance our career ambitions with the demands of being a parent, or with a longing for more free time in our lives?

The second question threading its way through this book is: how do we go about changing career and making the best possible decisions along the way? Although I offer no blueprint strategy that will work for everyone, there are three steps we ought to take. A starting point is to understand the sources of our confusions and fears about leaving our old jobs behind us and embarking on a new career. The next step is to reject the myth that there is a single, perfect job out there waiting for us to discover it, and instead identify our 'multiple selves' – a range of potential careers that might suit the different sides of our character. Finally, we have to turn the standard model of career change on its head: rather than meticulously planning then taking action, we should act first and reflect later, doing experimental projects that test-run our various selves in the real world. Ever thought of treating yourself to a 'radical sabbatical'?

To help answer these questions we will seek inspiration in the lives of famous figures, amongst them Leonardo da Vinci, Marie Curie and Anita Roddick. We will look for insights in the writings of philosophers, psychologists, sociologists and historians, and encounter practical – yet intellectually imaginative – activities to help clarify our thinking and narrow down the career options, such as writing a Personal Job Advertisement. We will draw lessons from the surprising stories of everyday workers, including a Belgian woman whose thirtieth-birthday present to herself was to try out thirty different careers in one year, and an Australian former fridge mechanic who found fulfilment by becoming an embalmer. I will also touch on some of my own career experiences and experiments, which have ranged from journalist to gardener, academic to community worker, with a smattering of telephone sales, tennis coaching and caring for young twins.

In a moment we'll launch our odyssey by exploring why it is so hard to decide which career path to follow. But before we do so, spend a few minutes thinking about the following question – or even better, discuss it with a friend:

- *What is your current work doing to you as a person – to your mind, character and relationships?*

2. A Short History of Career Confusion

'Blue Poles'

I remember, aged 23, standing with my father in front of *Blue Poles*, a painting by Jackson Pollock. He told me that the poles made him think of the bars of a prison cell into which he was gazing. My interpretation was the opposite. I felt as if I was trapped inside a cell, looking out in frustration at the free world.

'But how could you possibly feel that?' he asked. 'You have so much freedom and so many opportunities before you.'

Of course he was right. After graduating from university in Britain, I had travelled around Australia and Indonesia, earned some money working in telephone call centres, and volunteered at Amnesty International. Finally, I had found a job as a financial journalist in London – although it was not nearly as fulfilling as I'd hoped it would be.

'I feel I've got too many choices. All those squiggles on the canvas are my confused thoughts about what to do next. And the bars, maybe, are my fears about making the wrong decision. I don't think journalism is my true vocation in life. But how am I supposed to discover what is?'

'You're only young, kiddo. You can try different careers. There's no point doing something you don't really enjoy.'

It was well-meaning but bland advice that brought out my frustrations.

'You don't realize how hard it is to be free,' I replied brusquely, recognizing how pathetic it sounded as I said it.

He couldn't really understand. It made no sense to him that someone in my position could feel trapped. My father had arrived in Australia as a refugee from Poland in 1951, and had little opportunity to pursue his talents as a mathematician, linguist and musician. After serving three years as an auxiliary nurse in a Sydney hospital – forced labour that was the price of his citizenship – he was lucky to find a job as an accountant at IBM, which gave him the security and stability he needed to construct a new life following years of wartime dislocation. He worked there for over fifty years.

I, on the other hand, had career possibilities that he could never have hoped to imagine. And yet there I was complaining, in the National Gallery in Canberra, feeling perplexed – almost paralysed – by the array of choices before me. Should I try another branch of journalism? Or perhaps train as an English teacher and find a tutoring job in Spain or Italy? Maybe do tennis coaching for a while? Or a postgraduate degree? No matter how hard I stared at *Blue Poles*, I could not see any answers.

I am not alone in having experienced such swirls of confusion. Indeed, very few people today are able to shift career without going through a turbulent period of uncertainty about what direction to follow, which can last months – or even several years. Yet before focusing on how to make the best choices to find fulfilling work, we need to address a critical question: why is it so difficult to decide which career path to take? We must understand the sources of our confusion prior to seeking a way out of the labyrinth.

On some level the problem is plain overload. We can walk into a bookshop and find dozens of inch-thick career guides, each profiling hundreds of different jobs. One website lists 12,000 careers, starting with 487 under the letter 'A' alone – able seaman, abrasive grinder, absorption operator, acetone-recovery worker . . .[7] How are we supposed to choose between so many options? But beneath the sheer number of possibilities lie three fundamental reasons why career choice is often such a conundrum: we are not psychologically equipped to deal with the expansion of choice in recent history; we are burdened by our own pasts, especially the legacy of our early educational choices; and because the popular science of personality testing rarely helps us pinpoint fulfilling careers. As we gradually grasp how these forces shape our lives, we will discover that being able to identify the causes of our career dilemmas is the beginning of moving beyond them.

The Inheritance of Choice

In 1716, the ten-year-old Benjamin Franklin began working with his father as a tallow chandler in Boston. But after two years, the young boy was sick of cutting wicks and filling moulds for candles, and began dreaming of running away to sea, so his father thought to find him another career. They walked together around the neighbouring streets, where Benjamin could see the available options, watching joiners, bricklayers and other tradesmen at their work. Although Benjamin was 'still hankering for the sea', his father finally decided that his bookish son was best suited to becoming a printer, and so secured him an apprenticeship that legally bound him to a print workshop for the next nine years.[8]

For most of history, people had little choice about the jobs they did. Work was a matter of fate and necessity rather than freedom and choice. As with Benjamin Franklin, the decision was often made by their parents, and they were typically expected to follow the family trade. The occupational surnames that so many of us still carry, such as Smith, Baker and Butcher, are remnants of this tradition (Krznaric means 'son of a furrier' in Croatian). Many had the misfortune to be born into slavery or serfdom, and women were generally confined to work in the home. Since the industrial revolution, however, the range of career opportunities has expanded beyond recognition. We need to understand not only the origins of our new era of choice, but how we have become psychologically tyrannized by our hard-won freedom.

Karl Marx, one of the first social thinkers to take the subject of career choice seriously, saw that the erosion of feudalism and the rise of wage labour in the eighteenth and nineteenth centuries offered some hope for change. Each worker had 'become a free seller of labour-power, who carries his commodity wherever he finds a market'.[9] That sounds like progress. But he also pointed out that this was an illusory freedom, because most of the possibilities on offer were back-breaking industrial jobs that turned people into slaves of the capitalist system, 'which, vampire-like, lives only by sucking living labour'. If you were a poor woman in Britain, France or Belgium, for instance, you might be working in the coal mines as a 'drawer', crawling down the shafts on your hands and knees, and hauling up loads of coal to the surface for twelve hours a day, through tunnels less than thirty inches high.[10]

Working life before the rise of career choice in the Western world: a young girl at a spinning machine in North Carolina, photographed by Lewis Hine in 1908.

The nineteenth century may have been the era of Dickensian poverty and hellish labouring in the mines and textile mills, but it simultaneously witnessed a revolution in career choice through the spread of public education and the invention of the career open to talent. It was increasingly common, especially in northern Europe, for job selection to be based on merit and qualification rather than bloodline or social connections. Here at last was a chance to scramble up the social hierarchy – though you were most likely to benefit if you were a middle-class man. The British civil service, for example, began making appointments through competitive examination, a development which infuriated the aristocracy, who wanted the cushy jobs for themselves. Few outsiders were able to break into esteemed professions such as law, medicine or the clergy, but if you were the clever and hard-working son – or even daughter – of an artisan or labourer, you might now be able to find your way into white-collar work as an office clerk, tax collector or teacher. By 1851, there were 76,000 men and women working as school teachers in Britain, with a further 20,000 governesses.[11]

If the expansion of public education was the main event in the story of career choice in the nineteenth century, in the twentieth it was the growing number of women who entered the paid workforce. In the US in 1950 around 30 per cent of women had jobs, but by the end of the century that figure had more than doubled, a pattern which was repeated throughout the West.[12] This change partly resulted from the struggle for the vote and the legitimacy gained from doing factory work in two World Wars. Perhaps more significant was the impact of the pill. Within just fifteen years of its invention in 1955, over twenty million women were using oral contraceptives, with more than ten million using the coil.[13] By gaining more control over their own bodies, women now had greater scope to pursue their chosen professions without the interruption of unwanted pregnancy and childrearing. However, this victory for women's liberation has been accompanied by severe dilemmas for both women and men as they attempt to find a balance between the demands of family life and their career ambitions – a subject I will come back to.

In the twenty-first century, we stand as the inheritors of this gradual shift from fate to choice that has filtered into most Western nations. This is not to say that we now live in an age of enlightenment where everyone can, like Sylvester Stallone's boxing hero Rocky Balboa, achieve the mythical American Dream and become whoever they want to be, even if they were born on the wrong side of the tracks. Just ask the migrant workers on the checkout till at your local supermarket, or professional women trying to break into the upper echelons of the corporate world. But looking at the big historical picture, there is little doubt that the majority of people searching for a job today are likely to have far more career opportunities than if they had been living only a century ago.

To get a personal feel for this historical transformation, it is worth pausing to draw a family tree going back a few generations, and including the occupations of each of your family members. Now ask yourself this question:

- *How much choice have you had over your working life compared with your parents or grandparents?*

As in my own case, this family tree is likely to show the career options dwindling away as you go back in time. Perhaps your grandfather was proud to be a factory foreman, but he did not have the education to climb further up the ladder, and his career was disrupted by the war. Maybe your mother was one of the brightest girls in her class at school and wanted to go to university, but she succumbed to family and social pressure to marry young, have children and become a housewife. In all probability, you will have had the good fortune to enjoy many more opportunities than your forebears.

Yet if we are so lucky, why does choosing a career and finding fulfilling work still feel like such a challenge? The answer, according to psychologist Barry Schwartz, is that we now have *too much* choice, and are not good at dealing with it. Although a life without choice is almost unbearable, says Schwartz, we can reach a tipping point where having an abundance of options becomes an overload. 'At this point, choice no longer liberates, but debilitates. It might even be said to tyrannize.'[14]

In his book *The Paradox of Choice*, Schwartz begins by discussing our excess of consumer choice, noting that his local supermarket offers its customers 285 varieties of biscuit and 175 kinds of salad dressing. Another example he gives is the telephone industry. Unlike only a few decades ago, most people in affluent Western nations now have a choice of dozens of private telephone providers for their homes. But it can be extremely difficult to choose between the various companies, since they all offer different pricing systems, special deals and contract rules. Researching and weighing up the options can take hours. 'One effect of having so many options,' argues Schwartz, 'is that it produces paralysis rather than liberation – with so many options to choose from, people find it very difficult to choose at all.' Hence we frequently give up and stick with the telephone company we've already got. A second effect is that 'even if we manage to overcome the paralysis and make a choice, we end up less satisfied with the result of the choice than we would be if we had fewer options'. His main explanation for this apparent paradox is that we can always imagine having made a better choice, so we will regret the decision we did make, and thus feel unhappy about it.[15]

Schwartz believes that similar effects can arise in the realm of career decision-making, since we now have so many more options than in the past, having left behind the days of Benjamin Franklin.[16] Of course, choosing a job is different from shopping around for the right phone company or stereo system: we can't simply select the most enticing offer, since we are limited by factors such as our educational qualifications and work experience. Still, we may face dozens of possible pathways. Do you try to switch out of insurance broking into management consultancy, or maybe law or teaching, or move to a smaller firm, or spend a year travelling to clear your head? Or if you are thinking of retraining as a psychotherapist, will you take a course that focuses on psychodymanic, behavioural or cognitive approaches, or perhaps humanistic, person-centred or integrative? Being confronted by so many options can be a bewildering experience, as I remember when standing in front of *Blue Poles*. The consequence is that we often become psychologically paralysed, like a rabbit caught in the headlights. We get so worried about regretting making a bad choice that we may end up making no decision at all, and remain frozen in our current unfulfilling career.

Are there any solutions for dealing with the choice overload that afflicts modern society? Schwartz makes two main suggestions.

First, we should try to limit our options. So when we go shopping for new clothes, we could make a personal rule that we only visit two shops, rather than endlessly hunting for a better design or a better bargain. Second, we should 'satisfice more and maximize less'. What he means is that instead of aiming to buy the perfect pair of jeans, we should buy a pair that is 'good enough'. In other words, by lowering our expectations, we can avoid much of the angst and time-wasting that arises from having excessive choice.[17]

The problem, though, is that while such strategies might be helpful when shopping, they are inappropriate for making career decisions. There are no easy ways to limit the options – should we just look under the letter 'A' of a career guide? Moreover, the work we do is such a significant part of our lives, that 'good enough' is just not good enough. We should be striving for greater satisfaction rather than settling for less. What we really need to do is narrow down the choices by thinking more deeply about the core elements of a fulfilling career, and then devise concrete ways of testing out which of them best suit our aspirations. And that is precisely what the remaining chapters of this book are about.

The Perils of Education

Although cursed by the tyranny of excessive choice, many people are subject to a second force that makes it difficult to escape their unfulfilling jobs: they are bound by their own pasts, especially the educational choices made in their youth. We find ourselves following the furrows of a career track with origins deep in our personal histories, which can prevent us veering off in more adventurous directions.

It often begins in our school days. At the age of 15 or 16 we may embark on educational pathways that affect our working lives for years. This is commonly the case in Britain, where 80 per cent of pupils choose their A-level subjects for the final two years of high school on the basis of them 'being useful for their career'.[18] If you are thinking of being a foreign-language teacher, you might opt to take French, Italian and History. But having steered clear of the sciences, you can forget about ever becoming a doctor or a vet. Yet equally, if you decide to study medicine at college and manage to get the required entry grades, after slogging away for five or six years to qualify, the chances of you then deciding to become a graphic designer or session musician instead are virtually nil. Doctors might complain about the long hours and high stress, but they rarely ever switch careers out of the health sector.

The way that education can lock us into careers, or at least substantially direct the route we travel, would not be so problematic if we were excellent judges of our future interests and characters. But we are not. When you were 16, or even in your early twenties, how much did you know about what kind of career would stimulate your mind and offer a meaningful vocation? Did you even know the range of jobs that were out there? Most of us lack the experience of life – and of ourselves – to make a wise decision at that age, even with the help of well-meaning careers advisers.

The result is that people so often find themselves stuck in careers that do not suit their personalities, ideals or expectations. Their educational choices and opportunities have come to haunt them.

That is what happened to Sameera Khan, who we heard from earlier, who eventually wrenched herself away from a full-time position as a lawyer to try her hand as a social entrepreneur:

> Looking back now, it's crazy. At 16 I wanted to become a lawyer. How on earth am I supposed to know that that is what I want to do for the rest of my life? I'm not going to be the same person I am at 16 as I am at 45. I'm going to have different values, opinions and motivations.

Family pressures and expectations can also shape our early educational and job decisions, especially for the children of immigrants or those with high-achieving parents. One quarter of British Asian graduates feel their parents significantly influenced their career choice, a figure that is just one in ten for non-Asians. And these parents have very clear ideas about what is an appropriate profession for their offspring: 24 per cent favour medicine, 19 per cent law and 14 per cent accountancy.[19] Sameera fits the pattern: she knew choosing a career in law would please her Pakistani father and Indian mother. Unsurprisingly, they found her decision to resign from a high-paying legal job utterly perplexing. 'It's very difficult for them to comprehend,' she says. 'They would understand if I was older and had paid off most of the mortgage, and had kids and sent them to school. But they think I've rashly walked away from security, from setting myself up with a comfortable future, without gaining the financial benefits. Though in a way they're right – it makes me feel sick every time I think about what I've done.'

Although family opinion might shape our choices as impressionable youths, as we get older this influence gradually fades away.

Disapproval from her parents was not going to stop Sameera handing in her notice to her company as a thirty-two-year-old. But something else was. And that was the idea that she had spent so long studying to become a lawyer that it would be an unforgivable waste of those years if she left the profession: 'I thought that there was no way I would or could quit only a short time after qualifying – I'd worked so hard to get there. I would be letting myself down.' This kind of thinking resembles what economists describe as a decision based on 'sunk costs': if you buy an expensive pair of shoes that turn out to be incredibly uncomfortable, you won't want to throw them out because they cost you so much.[20] Similarly, you will be reluctant to give up a legal career to which you've dedicated a decade of your life, even if you find it unfulfilling. The sunk costs are just too high to ignore.

This sense that we might be squandering everything we have struggled to achieve is one of the greatest psychological barriers facing those contemplating career change. If you have spent years working your way up the ladder in law, advertising or any other profession, and then realize you are miserable and want to leave, you will hardly be consoled by a friend who reassures you that it was 'all part of life's journey' or that 'nothing is ever wasted'. They could be right in the end – the skills gained in your former career might be successfully applied elsewhere – yet such clichés won't make you feel much better at the time. You may also be unwilling to relinquish a work identity that gives you a sense of status and belonging. As already mentioned, Sameera worried that losing her identity as a lawyer would 'make me feel naked and completely empty'.

The upshot is that we can find ourselves in a constant struggle with our pasts, unable to make a decision to try something new because of an allegiance to the person we have been, rather than to the person we hope to become.

A helpful way to think about this is that we are caught between two forms of regret. On the one hand, the regret of abandoning a career into which we've put years of time, energy and emotion. And on the other, the possibility of looking back on our lives in old age and regretting that we didn't leave a job that was not offering us fulfilment. So which kind of regret should we give the greatest weight to in our decisions? The latter, according to the latest psychology research: the most emotionally corrosive form of regret occurs when we fail to take action on something that matters deeply to us. As time goes on, the choice we didn't make looms larger and larger in our minds, and the thought 'if only I had . . .' casts a dark shadow over our lives.[21] The philosopher A.C. Grayling has come to a similar conclusion: 'If there is anything worth fearing in the world, it is living in such a way that gives one cause for regret in the end.'

We ought to recognize that our early educational and career choices could well have been made when we were very different people than we are today. Clinging onto a job that no longer suits your personality or aspirations can be like trying to hold onto a relationship that just isn't working because you've grown apart. There comes a point when splitting up is probably the healthiest option, painful though it may be. We all change: we learn more about ourselves, and shift our priorities and perspectives, under the challenging tutelage of human experience.

- *What were the key moments in your education that shaped the direction of your career?*

The Flawed Science of Personality Testing

Faced by an overload of job options, and a reluctance to let go of our old career, how we are supposed to find our way out of the confusion? Over the past hundred years, an intriguing new profession has emerged, designed specifically to help us with this task: the career counsellor. Within an extraordinarily short period of time they have become the high priests of the modern workplace, offering expert advice to everyone from school leavers and college graduates to those who have just been made redundant or are subsumed in a mid-life crisis.

There are many varieties of career counselling, some extremely subtle and penetrating, others less so. One form deserves special attention, both because of its ubiquity and its potential dangers: career advice based on personality testing. The idea that you can fill out a standardized questionnaire and find a perfect match between your personality type and a particular career is an enticing one. But there is strong evidence to suggest that it is an essentially flawed method, which, although having some benefits, raises expectations that are rarely met. An important reason why the search for a fulfilling career can feel so difficult is because this apparently 'scientific' approach to career advice seldom provides the answers we had hoped for. To explain exactly why this is so, we need to return to the roots of career advice itself.

The so-called 'father of vocational guidance' was a former engineer, lawyer and school teacher named Frank Parsons. In 1908 he established the Vocation Bureau in Boston, which offered one of the world's first career-counselling services.[22] His seminal book, *Choosing a Vocation*, was published the following year, and became the bible for early generations of professional advisers, especially in the United States. Parsons firmly believed that career guidance should be based on scientific principles. He developed an elaborate system designed to match his clients' personality traits with the desired characteristics for success in specific industries. Walk into his office and he would begin by asking you no less than 116 assessment questions. He wanted to know not only your personal ambitions, strengths and weaknesses, but also how often you bathed and whether you slept with the window open. This man was thorough.

There was just one more thing he had to do before offering his sage advice for your working future. 'I carefully observe the shape of the applicant's head.' Yes, his head. 'If the applicant's head is largely developed behind the ears, with big neck, low forehead, and small upper head, he is probably of the animal type,' wrote Parsons, 'and should be dealt with on that basis'.[23]

Parsons was an adherent of the now-defunct 'science' of phrenology, which taught that a person's character could be assessed by measuring their cranial prominences and depressions. A twenty-two-year-old department-store assistant who came to see Parsons was observed to have a 'narrow head not very well balanced', and was advised against pursuing his ambition to become a lawyer. Others were luckier – 'head large, splendidly shaped,' he declared of the bookish son of an engineer.[24] Parsons was not alone in his cranial obsessions. One of the darker secrets of the history of career counselling is that it originated in the vogue for phrenology in the US in the nineteenth century, which itself had roots in racial theories suggesting that the superiority of whites over other races was evident in their finely shaped skulls. From the 1820s, writes one historian, 'many

'The boy – what will he become?' In this 1820s cartoon, a phrenologist measures the bumps on a young gentleman's head. Hanging on the wall is a portrait of Franz Josef Gall (1757–1828), founder of the popular pseudo-science.

job advertisements asked applicants to submit a phrenological report along with their letter of reference', and thousands were issued with career guidance based on their head measurements.[25]

This dubious scientific approach to career advice underwent a transformation in the first half of the twentieth century. Instead of measuring the outside of the head, the new trend was to measure the inside using personality tests, which had become increasingly popular since the French psychologist Alfred Binet invented the IQ test in 1905. By the 1970s, the issuing of psychometric tests to determine personality type had become part of the standard repertoire for many career counsellors.

The obvious question is whether such tests are successful at helping people identify a fulfilling career. My discussions with job seekers revealed a multitude of sceptics. Lisa Gormley, for example, remembers her reaction, aged 15, at reading the response to the personality questionnaire run at her high school:

> The computer printout told me that the best career match was being a dental nurse. It was a ridiculous suggestion. Dentists – urgh! – writing down 'upper left 1, 2, 3, 4, 5, 6 not present, 7, 8' while the dentist counts across some punter's teeth – boring! Being stuck inside a blue examining room with dusty slatted blinds on a sunny day – not for me, baby! I'm down the riverbank with a book of poetry . . . It stopped me thinking about careers altogether.

Lisa took pleasure in ignoring the advice. She went on to study philosophy and French at Oxford University, worked with refugees in Guatemala and Jordan, and later became an international human-rights lawyer.

We should not, however, be too quick to dismiss personality tests. There is a whole industry of career advisers who take them very seriously. Yet even the most sophisticated tests have considerable flaws. Take the Myers–Briggs Type Indicator (MBTI), the world's most popular psychometric test, which is based on Jung's theory of personality types. Over two million are administered every year, and there is a good chance you will have done one in a career-guidance session, during a management course at work, or as part of a job-interview process. The MBTI places you in one of sixteen personality types, based on dichotomous categories such as whether you are an introvert or an extrovert, or have a disposition towards being logical or emotional (what it calls 'thinking' or 'feeling').

The interesting – and somewhat alarming – fact about the MBTI is that, despite its popularity, it has been subject to sustained criticism by professional psychologists for over three decades.[26] One problem is that it displays what statisticians call low 'test-retest reliability'. So if you retake the test after only a five-week gap, there is around a 50 per cent chance that you will fall into a different personality category compared to the first time you took the test.[27] A second criticism is that the MBTI mistakenly assumes that personality falls into mutually exclusive 'either/or' categories. You are *either* an extrovert *or* an introvert, but never a mix of the two. Yet in reality, most people fall somewhere in the middle on this and other dimensions of personality.[28] If the MBTI also measured height, you would be classified as either tall or short, even though the majority of people are within a band of medium height. The consequence is that the test score of two people labelled respectively 'introvert' and 'extrovert' may be almost exactly the same, but they are placed by the MBTI into different categories since they fall just on either side of an imaginary dividing line.[29]

One other thing. And this really matters for readers of this book. According to official Myers–Briggs documents, the test can 'give you an insight into what kinds of work you might enjoy and be successful doing'. So if you are, like me, classified as 'INTJ' (your dominant traits are being introverted, intuitive and having a preference for thinking and judging), the best-fit occupations include management consultant, IT professional and engineer.[30] Would a change to one of these careers make me more fulfilled? Unlikely, according to respected US psychologist David Pittenger, because there is 'no evidence to show a positive relation between MBTI type and success within an occupation . . . nor is there any data to suggest that specific types are more satisfied within specific occupations than are other types'. Then why is the MBTI so popular? Its success, he argues, is primarily due to 'the beguiling nature of the horoscope-like summaries of personality and steady marketing'.[31]

Personality tests have their uses, even if they do not reveal any scientific 'truth' about us. If we are in a state of confusion they can be a great emotional comfort, offering a clear diagnosis of why our current job may not be right, and suggesting others that might suit us better. They also raise interesting hypotheses that aid self-reflection: until I took the MBTI, I had certainly never considered that IT could offer me a bright future (by the way, I apparently have the wrong personality type to be a writer). Yet we should be wary about relying on them as a magic pill that enables us suddenly to hit upon a dream career. That is why wise career counsellors treat such tests with caution, using them as only one of many ways of exploring who you are. Human personality does not neatly reduce into sixteen or any other definitive number of categories: we are far more complex creatures than psychometric tests can ever reveal. And as we will shortly learn, there is compelling evidence that we are much more likely to find fulfilling work by conducting career experiments in the real world than by filling out any number of questionnaires.[32]

Where does this journey into career confusion leave us? It should now be clear that you are not alone in the uncertainties you may feel about which path to follow, nor are you personally to blame for them. History has bequeathed us an overload of options that few of us are psychologically equipped to handle. We might also be struggling against the legacies of educational and career decisions made in our immature youths or under family pressure. What is more, the promise of 'scientific' career advice, which maps our personalities onto specific jobs, has failed to materialize and offer an easy way out of our dilemmas.

You should also be in a better position to answer the central questions underlying your own career confusions. Give yourself ten minutes to consider them right now. On a sheet of paper, write down – or describe in pictures and diagrams – your responses to the following:

- *What are the three main reasons why you are feeling confused about where to go next?*
- *What are your three greatest fears about changing career?*
- *What are the three biggest practical challenges you face?*

I will be saying much more about how to confront our fears and other obstacles, but for the moment it is simply useful to think about these questions, identifying your worries and looking them in the eye.

We are now poised to move beyond the realm of uncertainties. We need to boldly go where most personality tests fail to take us, and explore exactly what kinds of fulfilment we wish to seek in our careers. Do we want to follow the glittering allure of money and status, or to be guided in our search for meaning by our values, talents and passions?

3. Giving Meaning to Work

The Five Dimensions of Meaning

The most terrible punishment for any human being, wrote Dostoyevsky, would be if they were condemned to a lifetime of work that was 'completely and utterly devoid of usefulness and meaning'. He was right that meaning matters. Along with flow and freedom, it is one of the three basic ingredients of a fulfilling career. But he leaves us wondering what meaning really *means*, and how to find it.

In this chapter I want to consider five different aspects of what can make a job meaningful: earning money, achieving status, making a difference, following our passions, and using our talents. We can think about these as the fundamental motivating forces that drive people in their careers. They are the psychological underpinnings of the work we do, and why we do it. Both money and status are known as 'extrinsic' motivating factors, since they are about approaching work as a means to an end, whereas the remaining three are 'intrinsic', with the work valued as an end in itself.[33]

The question we need to address is: Which of these motivations should be the principal guide in our career decisions? Should we, for instance, prefer a job with an excellent pay package over one with a lower salary but which provides greater scope for using our creative talents? Clarifying our thoughts on where our priorities lie can help us develop a personal vision of what meaningful work looks like, so we can narrow down the career possibilities and make the right choices.

As we explore each motivation in turn, we will discover not only their individual challenges and the tensions between them, but that there is no single blueprint for a meaningful career. Yet it will also become clear that pursuing a career mainly because it offers the tempting rewards of money and status is an unlikely route to the good life. With the help of a cosmetics tycoon, a professional athlete and a former space-flight engineer, we will learn that following our values, passions and talents is the most likely way to satisfy our hunger for fulfilment. At that point, we will be sufficiently primed to try three imaginative activities designed to generate concrete career options.

Money and the Good Life

Is one of the main reasons you're in your current job because the money is good? And is one of the main reasons you are reluctant to leave it because you can't imagine taking a substantial salary cut, or entering a profession with limited financial prospects? When I ask these questions in the classes I teach at The School of Life on 'How to Find a Job you Love', at least half the people in the room sheepishly raise their hands.

Their response is unsurprising, because choosing a career for its monetary rewards is the oldest and most powerful motivation in the world of work. In the nineteenth century, the German philosopher Arthur Schopenhauer suggested why this desire for money is so pervasive: 'Men are often criticized that money is the chief object of their wishes and is preferred above all else, but it is natural and even unavoidable. For money is an inexhaustible Proteus, ever ready to change itself into the present object of our changeable wishes and manifold needs . . . Money is human happiness in the abstract.' So does this mean we should place our hopes for career fulfilment in substantial salaries and big bonuses? The answer is no.

Schopenhauer may have been right that the desire for money is widespread, but he was wrong on the issue of equating money with happiness. Overwhelming evidence has emerged in the last two decades that the pursuit of wealth is an unlikely path to achieving personal wellbeing – the ancient Greek ideal of *eudaimonia* or 'the good life'. The lack of any clear positive relationship between rising income and rising happiness has become one of the most powerful findings in the modern social sciences. Once our income reaches an amount that covers our basic needs, further increases add little, if anything, to our levels of life satisfaction.[34]

This is because we typically get caught on what psychologist Martin Seligman calls a 'hedonic treadmill': as we get richer and accumulate more material possessions, our expectations rise, so we work even harder to earn money to buy more consumer goods to boost our wellbeing, but then our expectations rise once more, and on it goes.[35] We shift from a standard TV to widescreen, from one car to two, from renting a holiday home to owning a second home, and none of it does much to boost our sense of having a fulfilling and meaningful life, and may well contribute to higher levels of anxiety and depression since we are forever yearning for more. Few people have the conviction to avoid the hedonic treadmill, even those who promise themselves they will only stay in a soulless big-money job for a limited period such as five years before getting out: they almost always get caught on the treadmill and fail to keep their promise.

Amongst the wisest commentators on such matters is the psychotherapist Sue Gerhardt, who in her book *The Selfish Society* observes:

> In the West, we are trapped in these cycles of endless striving and dissatisfaction, trying to keep up with the ever-more elaborate displays of consumption we see on television and on the internet. This drive to accumulate material goods and services appears to have addictive qualities: it is a powerful appetite which has no inbuilt mechanism to alert us to when we have had enough; we want more and more – especially, it seems, just that little bit more than everyone else . . . Although we have relative material abundance, we do not in fact have emotional abundance. Many people are deprived of what really matters. Lacking emotional security, they seek security in material things.[36]

So we may be looking for fulfilment in the wrong places – in *having* rather than *being*, in accumulating possessions rather than in building nurturing, empathic relationships. It might be time to abandon the assumption that a career mainly driven by making money can buy us the purposeful, flourishing lives that we so dearly desire.

Furthermore, when people are asked about what gives them job satisfaction, they rarely place money at the top of the list. In the Mercer global-engagement scale – drawing on interviews with thousands of workers in Europe, the US, China, Japan and India – 'base pay' only comes in at number seven out of twelve key factors. What really seems to matter to people is the quality of their relationships in the workplace: both 'respect' and 'the people you work with' head up the list. Other polls similarly reveal that good relationships with colleagues, as well as issues such as work–life balance, job security and sense of autonomy trump pay as a source of satisfaction.[37]

Few people are likely to completely ignore money when making a career decision: we all have mortgages hanging over us, bills to pay, and families to care for. The real issue is how much weight we should assign to it. We don't need philosophers or spiritual gurus to tell us the answer. There is now abundant empirical evidence to suggest that if we truly aspire to live the good life, then we would be rash to allow money to be our primary goal.

- *What would you most like to change about your attitude to money?*

Status and the Secrets of Embalming

Apart from money, the other extrinsic reward people commonly seek is social status. This comes in two varieties. One is the status we get from having a prestigious job which is admired and revered by others, such as being a diplomat, television producer, barrister, surgeon, professional athlete, professor or writer. It's an alluring prospect: as one of my students recently told me, 'I've always wanted a job that sounded cool to my friends.' Like the ancient Romans, we still have a strong yearning for reputation and glory.

The second variety is status based on our position relative to others. This partly reveals itself in our income preferences. A famous study in behavioural economics showed that if given a choice between earning $50,000 a year with everyone else earning $25,000, or earning $100,000 while others earned $200,000, the majority of people would choose the former.[38] We also care about our relative position in career hierarchies. If you see all your peers climbing the ladder of success, becoming company directors or top managers, yet you remain languishing at the bottom of the ranks, then you may well feel something of a failure and have a desire to join them.

Status can be an important way to boost our self-esteem. But as the eighteenth-century philosopher Jean-Jacques Rousseau warned, 'this universal desire for reputation', in which we judge ourselves through other people's eyes, is fraught with dangers.[39] We can easily find ourselves pursuing a career that society considers prestigious, but which we are not intrinsically devoted to ourselves – one that does not fulfil us on a day-to-day basis. In my teaching, I am constantly meeting people who are deeply unhappy about their work despite having apparently enviable careers, such as being a photojournalist or neuroscientist. Others in the room can hardly believe that they are miserable in their outwardly impressive jobs.

There is a further problem. Once we achieve one status level, another often instantly appears above it. We may aspire, for instance, to be a successful TV producer. But having become the producer of a popular TV show, we might then want to be amongst those who have won coveted awards or who also make feature films. Our peer group shifts, and the status we seek is forever just beyond our grasp, much like the 'hedonic treadmill' that continually raises our expectations as consumers. The writer and spiritual thinker C.S. Lewis identified this problem when he said that most of us desire to be a member of an 'inner ring' of esteemed or important people, but we 'will reach no "inside" that is worth reaching' since there are always more rings within it.[40] The lesson may be the simple one that we should not be so concerned about what other people think about us.

- *Who do you imagine is judging your status – perhaps family, old friends or colleagues? Do you want to grant them that power?*

Of course, most of us do want recognition from others. But how can we gain it, if not through status? The answer lies in a funeral parlour.

Trevor Dean used to work as a refrigeration mechanic, and later as a shop assistant, in the Australian state of Victoria. One day, a friend mentioned that he was doing work experience at a local mortuary. Trevor, who was accustomed to seeing death, having spent years as a volunteer fire-fighter, found himself quizzing his friend about what sounded like a fascinating career:

> I wanted a job that had meaning, that was challenging, and that was interesting. So when a local ad appeared for a funeral assistant, I went for it and out of thirty applicants, I was the lucky one. Three years later I applied to do the embalmers course. I'm now fully qualified and have never looked back. The study made me realize how incredible this human body of ours is.
>
> What does the job mean to me? I look after loved ones on their last journey; I care for them as if they were my own. I have a folder full of thank-you letters from family members, which I think explain a lot about why I am an embalmer.

> One letter says, 'his wife just kept saying how peaceful and beautiful he looked and wanted to pass on her thanks'. Another that, 'the family were absolutely rapt with the way she was presented and couldn't stop raving about how good she looked, so thank you for your work.' A third says, 'the friends of ___ have said that he looked "bloody fantastic", you've done a great job my friend!'

The sense of fulfilment that Trevor clearly derives from his work is not based on having a high-status job: being an embalmer is hardly a prestigious profession. As Trevor himself recognizes, 'The West fears death, and nine out of ten people really do freak out when I tell them I'm an embalmer.' What makes his job so worthwhile is that it gives him respect.

By respect I don't mean being treated with deference by others, like some big-time Mafia boss. What I mean is being appreciated for what we personally bring to a job, and being valued for our individual contribution. In Trevor's case, that sense of respect comes from family members of the deceased, who value his skills as an embalmer. More commonly, we might gain our respect from work colleagues who praise us for our creative intellect or organizational genius.

While most of us wish to enjoy a dose of social status, the feeling that we are respected by others for what we do and how we do it is one of the keys to having a meaningful career. As the sociologist of work Richard Sennett explains, respect enables us to feel like 'a full human being whose presence matters'.[41] No wonder it ranks so high in surveys of job satisfaction. The lesson is that in our quest for fulfilling work, we should seek a job that offers not just good status prospects, but good respect prospects. That may mean avoiding large bureaucratic organisations where individual efforts are barely acknowledged, and finding a workplace where employees feel treated as unique human beings and part of a community of equals. Who knows, you might even discover yourself working in a funeral home.

I Want to Make a Difference

'I want to make a difference' is a phrase that can be heard amongst recent graduates wandering the caverns of university careers offices, and equally amongst thirty-something professionals who feel frustrated that they spend most of their days dealing with tedious emails or marketing products they don't really care about. They want something more: to make a positive contribution to people and planet, and to put their values into practice. It is an increasingly common desire, even in our age of rampant hyper-individualism, and one that resembles the ancient Greeks' aspiration to perform some virtuous and noble deed that would give their lives a sense of purpose and ensure their immortality in historical memory.[42] We want to be able to look back in old age and feel that we have left our mark.

Most people intuitively know that making a difference is a promising path to a fulfilling career. And it's borne out by the evidence. A major study of ethical work by Howard Gardner, Mihaly Csikszentmihalyi and William Damon showed that those doing what they call 'good work' – defined as 'work of expert quality that benefits the broader society' – consistently exhibit high levels of job satisfaction.[43] The moral philosopher Peter Singer would agree. He argues that our greatest hope for personal fulfilment is dedicating our lives – and if possible our *working* lives – to a 'transcendent cause' that is larger than ourselves, especially an ethical one such as animal rights, poverty alleviation or environmental justice.[44] Such views build on deep traditions of religious thought that promote the idea that giving to others through our work is spiritually uplifting. As Martin Luther King said, 'Everybody can be great because everybody can serve.'

The question is how to go about it. People often assume that ethical careers are mainly found in charities or the public sector; say working at a homeless shelter or as a special-needs teacher in a state school. But one of the great revolutions of the modern workplace is that there are now so many more career opportunities for making a difference, as Clare Taylor discovered.

After graduating with a degree in engineering science, Clare found a job in an engineering consultancy in San Francisco, then moved to a better-paid position in a small software house. While busy working on building content-management systems for Sony, so people could get their soap-opera updates online, she began moonlighting for a media organisation called Internews, helping Palestinians use the internet to spread news of the violence they were experiencing. That's when she had a moment of political revelation, realizing that she cared much more about social justice than boosting Sony's corporate profits. 'I had an epiphany,' said Clare. 'I suddenly knew which side I was on.'

So she ditched her dotcom job and returned home to Ireland to start a new life. Appalled by the materialistic money-grabbing of the Celtic Tiger boom, she decided to take a risk and do something about it:

> With no publishing experience, I used the last of my savings to start a magazine with the aim of changing the culture. It was called *YOKE: Free Thinking for the World Citizen.* It lasted two years, gained a fair bit of media attention and some great contributors, including Isabel Allende, Pico Iyer and Jeanette Winterson. I was living on the dole and in a bedsit, running the magazine from my office which was under the loft bed in the corner of the room. Although I was skint, I had a real sense that this was exactly what I was supposed to be doing.

Clare had to close the magazine when she became pregnant. Since then she has worked for an NGO on the economics of sustainability, for a government agency on renewable-energy policy, and has been a researcher for television programmes about sustainable development. Although not certain where she'll go next, Clare remains committed to the struggle against what she calls 'the death march of consumerism':

> My career search has cost in financial terms but the experience has enriched my life. Personally, I couldn't work for a cause that I didn't believe in – this is a very big part of meaningful work for me. I was once talking to a friend of my father's about life choices and the awkward translation of ideas into reality. He told me that life was short and I must use it to do the things I was born to do. The next day he died of a heart attack. Our time here is short and we must be willing to take risks and make fools of ourselves, but never give up hope of a better world. The stakes are so much higher than any of the status or money rewards of the rat race.

Clare's efforts to make a difference have taken her from online journalism and literary publishing to ecological campaigning, public-policy work and television. That's a lot more varied than would have been possible a century ago, when ethical careers were largely limited to missionary work and a few professions like nursing. But whichever paths we may choose to follow, there are two challenges that anybody hoping to make a difference will have to face.

The first concerns the impact of their actions. One of the greatest frustrations is that it is often difficult to see, in concrete terms, what difference your work is actually making. I know this from personal experience, having spent years as an academic and development consultant writing about poverty and human rights in Latin America. Were all those words I was churning out really helping to improve people's day-to-day lives? I felt much better when I made a major career change and started running a community project in my home town of Oxford, where the effects of my work were far more visible. But then I worried that I wasn't making a difference on a broad enough scale.

A second challenge is the tensions that can arise between making a difference and making money. In Clare Taylor's experience, doing work that embodies her values has involved a clear financial sacrifice. But the emergence of new economic sectors such as social enterprise raises the question of whether it might be possible to enjoy both the intrinsic rewards of being true to our beliefs and the extrinsic rewards of earning money. The career of Anita Roddick, founder of The Body Shop cosmetics chain, can help us dissect these issues.

By the time of her death in 2007, Roddick was one of the world's most successful and admired entrepreneurs, famous for having brought ethics into enterprise. But The Body Shop didn't start out

Anita Roddick in the early days of The Body Shop in the 1970s. She came to believe in 'the necessity of reinventing work by attaching a values system to it'.

as a values-driven business. When she founded the first store in Brighton in 1976 – after failed ventures running a bed & breakfast and a rock'n'roll burger bar – Roddick was merely trying to make enough money to survive on. She asked customers to return their bottles for refilling not for environmental reasons but for financial ones. 'Everything was determined by money, or rather a lack of it', she wrote in her memoirs.[45]

Gradually, however, values started filtering into the business, transforming The Body Shop into a company geared to making a difference as well as making face creams, and which earned profits while not intent on maximizing them. 'I am opposed to maximizing profits to satisfy investors,' Roddick stated bluntly. Instead, at the heart of the company's philosophy was 'the necessity of reinventing work by attaching a values system to it . . . we're a hair and skin company that works for positive social change'.

What did this mean in practice? An early initiative, working together with her husband Gordon, was to use their fleet of lorries to promote social causes, like pasting pictures of missing persons on the side of the trucks with a helpline number. Within weeks they had received 30,000 calls and several of the people were found. In 1988 they established Soapworks, a soap factory-cum-social enterprise in a deprived area of Glasgow, which funnelled profits back into the local community. In 1991, seed money from The Body Shop Foundation was used to start up the *Big Issue*, a magazine sold by homeless people, which now exists in eight nations and sells 300,000 copies a week. The Body Shop also pioneered fair-trade relationships, working with indigenous communities in Brazil and other countries to directly source ingredients for their products. Roddick later used the company as a political machine to campaign for the rights of the Ogoni people, whose lives were being destroyed by Shell's oil drilling in the Niger Delta.[46]

Throughout these decades, Roddick's sense of fulfilment in her job – and the fulfilment enjoyed by many of her employees – grew out of the company's radical socio-political agenda. So we might conclude that private enterprise offers enormous potential to those who seek a purposeful, values-based career. Not so fast. Even someone as brilliant and charismatic – and domineering – as Roddick could not survive without making serious ethical compromises.

'One of the biggest mistakes I made was to go public and on the stock market,' she admitted.[47] After doing so, growing obligations to shareholders, investors and corporate management began to eat away at the moral fibre of The Body Shop. The problems emerged in the early nineties when top management opposed her campaign against the Persian Gulf War, arguing that it would damage sales. Consultants were brought in to restructure the company and make it more profitable, reducing the scope for social initiatives.[48] Once Roddick stepped down from being CEO in the late nineties – some say she was pushed out – The Body Shop lost its ethical drive. Today, the company is part of the L'Oréal corporate group, and barely pays lip service to the values it once possessed.

It is a salutary tale, revealing the potential discord that can emerge when trying both to make money and to make a difference: enterprise and ethics do not easily mix.

Rather than hoping to create a harmonious union between the pursuit of money and values, we might have better luck trying to combine values with talents. This idea comes courtesy of Aristotle, who is attributed with saying, 'Where the needs of the world and your talents cross, there lies your vocation.' That may be the single most useful piece of career advice to have emerged in the past 3,000 years, and one with which Anita Roddick would probably have agreed. We might all contemplate turning our particular gifts and abilities towards the major social, political and ecological dilemmas of our age. Although we may believe that there are no ethical careers that can easily accommodate our talents or expertise, almost any professional skill can be applied in a job that makes a difference: we can use our marketing prowess working for a fast-food chain or for a cancer-research foundation; we can offer our accounting experience to an investment bank or a mental-health charity. Ultimately, the choice is ours.

- *Where do your talents meet the needs of the world?*

How to Cultivate Passions and Talents

While an ethical career is one intrinsically rewarding path to the good life, there is also the option of focusing on your passions and talents. Forget money, status or even making a difference: do what you love and what you're really good at. In all my years of talking to people about their jobs, I've never come across a better example of this than Wayne Davies.

For over two decades Wayne, who grew up in Australia, was a professional coach and player of the esoteric medieval sport of 'real tennis'. The forerunner of regular tennis, real tennis is played on an indoor court where the ball can ricochet off the walls and points are won by hitting targets. There are only forty-five courts and 5,000 players worldwide (I happen to be one of them). Wayne was so enamoured with real tennis when he first discovered it in 1978 that within months he resigned his job as a secondary-school science teacher, took a huge salary cut, and began a new career as an assistant coach in Melbourne. He had to travel for almost three hours each morning to arrive at work by 8 a.m. I once asked him what was the best thing about being a real tennis pro. 'Playing tennis,' he replied, as if I had asked a very stupid question. He immediately went on. 'What's the best thing about life? Playing tennis. That's what I think. Life is a tennis court. I'm never happier than when I'm playing a proper match – you can erase everything else in life.'

After becoming the head professional at the real tennis club in New York City, Wayne gave his whole life to the game, sleeping on a mattress at the club so he could get up and practise at dawn for four hours before his coaching work started for the day. He sometimes even practised in the middle of the night in his pyjamas. 'If you're going to get good at anything,' he told me, 'you've got to have tunnel vision.' This was a man obsessed, even possessed. The result? He became the sport's world champion in 1987, reigning undefeated for almost eight years.[49]

Two things made Wayne so fulfilled by his career, apart from the glory of his tournament victories. First, he felt he was realizing his potential as an athlete, stretching his talents as far as they would go. Second, he had merged his greatest passion with his work. Following the latter strategy, however, is a controversial choice. While some people swear that transforming their hobbies or interests into their jobs was the turning point on the road to fulfilment, others claim that it was a terrible mistake. You might love building model trains, but starting up a company selling them online, with all the stresses involved, could drain all the joy from your passion, and make you nostalgic for those rainy Sunday afternoons tinkering with engines, when you had no sales figures to worry about.

This is a subject I will address further when discussing freedom, but on balance I think mixing work and play is usually worth the risk of potential contamination. As the cultural critic Pat Kane argues, we should strive to develop a 'play ethic' in our lives, which places 'yourself, your passions and enthusiasms at the centre of your world'.[50] The French writer François-René de Chateaubriand made a similar point over a century ago:

> A master in the art of living draws no sharp distinction between his work and his play; his labour and his leisure; his mind and his body; his education and his recreation. He hardly knows which is which. He simply pursues his vision of excellence through whatever he is doing, and leaves others to determine whether he is working or playing. To himself, he always appears to be doing both.

There is a further dilemma awaiting those intent on pursuing their talents or passions in the workplace, which is whether we should aim to be specialists, directing ourselves towards a single profession, or aim to become generalists, developing our various talents and passions across several different fields. I think of this as the question of whether we should aspire to be high achievers or 'wide achievers'.

For over a century, Western culture has been telling us that the best way to use our talents and be successful is to specialize and become an expert in a narrow field, just like Wayne Davies. This ideology is to a significant extent rooted in the division of labour that emerged during the industrial revolution, which split most jobs into tiny segments in order to increase efficiency and production levels. So now many people find themselves funnelled into working in a limited field, for instance as a corporate-tax specialist, reference librarian or anaesthetist.[51] Specialization may be all very well if you happen to have skills particularly suited to these jobs, or if you are passionate about a niche area of work, and of course there is also the benefit of feeling pride in being considered an expert. But there is equally the danger of becoming dissatisfied by the repetition inherent in many specialist professions: studies of surgeons reveal that those who only perform operations on tonsils or appendices soon begin to feel the tedium and become unhappy in their lucrative jobs.[52]

Moreover, our culture of specialization conflicts with something most of us intuitively recognize, but which careers advisers are only beginning to understand: we each have multiple selves. According to Herminia Ibarra, one of the world's leading academic thinkers on career change:

> our working identity is not a hidden treasure waiting to be discovered at the very core of our being – rather, it is made up of many possibilities . . . we are many selves.[53]

Indeed, we need not think that being, say, a secondary-school English teacher is the only career that could bring us fulfilment. We have complex, multi-faceted experiences, interests, values and talents, which might mean that we could also find fulfilment as a web designer, or a community police officer, or running an organic cafe.

This is a potentially liberating idea with radical implications. It raises the possibility that we might discover career fulfilment by escaping the confines of specialization and cultivating ourselves as wide achievers. Only then may we be able to develop the many sides of who we are, allowing the various petals of our identity to fully unfold. There are two classic approaches to being a wide achiever: becoming a 'Renaissance generalist', who pursues several careers simultaneously, or a 'serial specialist', who does one after another.

The first option is modelled on the Renaissance ideal that to be fully human we should do all we can to foster the array of our individual talents and the many dimensions of our personality. Perhaps the greatest Renaissance generalist of them all was Leonardo da Vinci. He was not only a painter, but also an engineer, inventor, natural scientist, philosopher and musician. Open his notebooks and you will see jottings on an incredible variety of subjects: there are anatomical sketches of horses, plans for flying machines, investigations of human foetuses, astronomical observations, designs for theatrical costumes, fossil studies, to name but a few. As the art critic Kenneth Clark put it, Leonardo was 'the most relentlessly curious man in history'.[54] In terms of his working life, it meant that in the same week he might be creating a war machine for a power-hungry duke, doing a portrait for an artistic patron, and studying cloud movements on the side. History has never seen a more accomplished wide achiever.

Leonardo was an early example of what is today known as a 'portfolio worker', a term invented by management thinker Charles Handy.

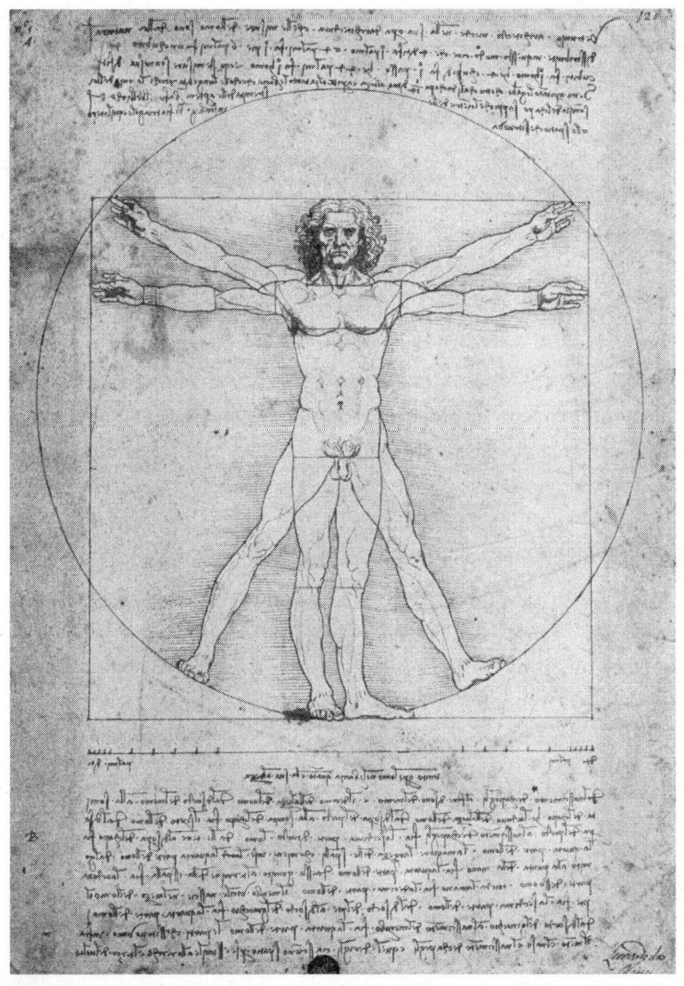

Leonardo's *Vitruvian Man*, arms stretched out wide, is the quintessential symbol of the Renaissance wide achiever.

A portfolio worker develops a range or 'portfolio' of careers, each of which they do part-time, and possibly on a freelance basis. So you might work as a development economist three days a week, then spend the rest of the week as a self-employed wedding photographer or online book dealer. Or you may wish to stretch both mind and body, dividing your time between being a software programmer and a ballet teacher. Handy believed that this was a smart survival strategy in turbulent economic times, reducing the risks of unemployment. But we need not think about portfolio working only in such negative terms. Adopting the more positive Renaissance perspective, pursuing several careers at the same time is a way of thriving and being true to our multiple selves.

Becoming a Renaissance generalist provides plenty of challenges, not least amongst them the prospect of financial insecurity if you are juggling freelance jobs – an issue I will return to. So you might feel more comfortable indulging your various talents and passions by becoming a serial specialist. Instead of pursuing several careers concurrently, we might imagine having three or four very different careers in succession – perhaps starting in public relations, followed by running a youth hostel, then becoming a self-employed gardener. This approach to being a wide achiever makes sense in a world where the retirement age keeps shifting back and working lives are getting longer: there is more space in which to fit several careers. Even making one substantial career change can free us from a profession that has lost its attractions and allow us to explore other sides of who we are.

Consider the example of Lisa Brideau, a former aerospace engineer who did contract work on design projects for NASA. A few years after discovering that space-flight engineering was not nearly as exciting as she thought it would be, and feeling that she wasn't particularly good at the job, Lisa was looking out for something new:

> It turned out that the answer was all around me, in the horrifying suburbs of Wisconsin I had been living in: urban planning. The existence of soulless urban sprawl enraged me to such a degree that I had to do something about it. It was mostly a blind leap. I read some books on the subject, sat in on an urban-geography course at the local university, then applied to some graduate planning schools. After getting my Masters, I went to work in the planning department of a very progressive city. I've had to work my way up the ranks, but that's just given me more time to learn my craft. So far urban planning is awesome – it's endlessly fascinating.
>
> I was lucky to have the financial resources to go back to studying, but what really made career change easy for me was that I never thought I'd have just one career. There are so many interesting things out there – why do just one forever? I think everyone should up and quit their job at least once in their life.

Lisa is a natural serial specialist. Her idea of shifting career at least once might be wise advice, especially because, as we have already discovered, our motivations and ambitions evolve throughout the course of our lives, and we are often poor judges of our future interests. The route of a serial specialist may be just what we need to nurture our many talents and passions, and to lead the many lives that lay dormant within us, like seeds beneath the snow.

- *What would being a wide achiever encompass for you?*

Imagining Your Many Selves

Having explored the various motivations that offer meaning, it seems that the prize of meaningful work goes to those who pursue intrinsically rewarding jobs that make a difference, use their talents or reflect their passions – or that involve some intoxicating combination of the three. Although we all desire money and status to some degree, a career decision driven primarily by these extrinsic motivations is unlikely to offer sublime depths of meaning to our lives.

Now we need to get practical, and use what we have learned about these five motivating factors to help generate concrete employment options that could provide a fulfilling, life-enhancing career. This is not a matter of finding that unique dream job which ticks all the boxes – that's a mythological ideal we would be wise to abandon. Rather, it is about identifying a range of possibilities reflecting our multiple selves, which we can later 'test out' in reality. Here are three activities, which build on one another, that I recommend you do to help with this task.

The Map of Choices

The first, called the Map of Choices, is designed to enable you to reflect on where you've come from, before you focus on where you're going. You start by spending ten minutes drawing a map of your career path so far. It can take any form – a zigzagging line, a branching tree or maybe a labyrinth. On this map you should indicate not only the jobs you have done, but the different motivations and forces that have shaped your route. If a major career decision was influenced by the prospect of more money or status, show it on your map – similarly if you were driven by your talents, passions or values. You should also add other factors that might have guided you, such as the role played by your educational choices, parental expectations, professional career advice or chance. Even if you've only ever held one job, try mapping out what drew you into it.

Having created your artwork, now spend another ten minutes looking at it and thinking about these three questions.

- *What does your map reveal about your overall approach to your working life so far? There may be general patterns you can see, such as the way you never stay in a position for more than a couple of years, or that you seem to have fallen into most jobs rather than really choosing them.*
- *Which of the following motivations have you given greatest priority to in your career choices: money, status, respect, passions, talents or making a difference? (rank them from greatest to least priority)*
- *Which two of the motivations mentioned above do you most want to shape your career choices in the future, and why?*

Make a note of your responses, ready for the next activity.

Imaginary Lives

Imaginary Lives is a thought experiment I have adapted from two important career-change thinkers, Julia Cameron and John Williams, which aims to take your ideas a stage closer towards specific job options.[55] It's simple but potentially powerful.

- *Imagine five parallel universes, in each of which you could have a whole year off to pursue absolutely any career your desired. Now think of five different jobs you might want to try out in each of these universes.*

Be bold in your thinking, have fun with your ideas and your multiple selves. Your five choices might be food photographer, member of parliament, tai chi instructor, social entrepreneur running a youth education project, and wide-achieving Renaissance generalist. One person I know who did this activity – a documentary film maker who was having doubts about her career – listed massage therapist, sculptor, cellist, screenplay writer, and owner of her own bar on a tiny, old-fashioned Canarian island.

Now come back down to earth and look hard at your five choices. Write down what it is about them that attracts you. Then look at them again, and think about this question:

- *How does each career measure up against the two motivations in the previous activity that you chose to prioritize in the future?*

If you decided, for instance, that you want a combination of making a difference and high status, check whether your five imaginary careers might provide them. The point is to help you think more deeply about exactly what you are looking for in a career, the kind of experiences that you truly desire.

The Personal Job Advertisement

These two activities are likely to have encouraged some clearer ideas about genuine career possibilities, but you should not assume that you are necessarily the best judge of what might offer you fulfilment. Writing a Personal Job Advertisement allows you to seek the advice of other people.

The concept behind this task is the opposite of a standard career search: imagine that newspapers didn't advertise jobs, but rather advertised people who were looking for jobs.

You do it in two steps. First, write a half-page job advertisement that tells the world who you are and what you care about in life. Put down your talents (e.g. you speak Mongolian, can play the bass guitar), your passions (e.g. ikebana, scuba diving), and the core values and causes you believe in (e.g. wildlife preservation, women's rights). Include your personal qualities (e.g. you are quick-witted, impatient, lacking self-confidence). And record anything else that is important to you – a minimum salary or that you want to work abroad. Make sure you *don't* include any particular job you are keen on, or your educational qualifications or career background. Keep it at the level of underlying motivations and interests.

Here comes the intriguing part. Make a list of ten people you know from different walks of life and who have a range of careers – maybe a policeman uncle or a cartoonist friend – and email them your Personal Job Advertisement, asking them to recommend two or three careers that might fit with what you have written. Tell them to be specific – for example, not replying 'you should work with children' but 'you should do charity work with street kids in Rio de Janeiro'.

You will probably end up with an eclectic list of careers, many of which you would never have thought of yourself. The purpose is not only to give you surprising ideas for future careers, but also to help you see your many possible selves.

After doing these three activities, and having explored the various dimensions of meaning, you should feel more confident about making a list of potential careers that offer the promise of meaningful work. What should you do next? Certainly not begin sending out your CV. Rather, as the following chapter explains, the key to finding a fulfilling career is to experiment with these possibilities in that rather frightening place called the real world. It's time to take a 'radical sabbatical'.

4. Act First, Reflect Later

In Search of Courage

In 1787, the pioneering feminist thinker Mary Wollstonecraft left her position as a governess for a wealthy family in Ireland and set out on a precarious career as a writer, at a moment in history when almost no women were professional authors. In 1882, Paul Gauguin gave up his steady and successful job as a stockbroker in Paris to become a full-time artist. At the age of 30, Albert Schweitzer left behind his glittering career as an organist and theological scholar in Strasbourg to retrain as a doctor, travelling to the African tropics in 1913 to establish a leper hospital.

While some people are inspired by such stories of bold career change, they may make others feel inadequate, even intimidated. Why? Because although we might dream of changing our jobs, we so often lack the courage to do so. Half the workforce in the Western world is dissatisfied with their careers, but around a quarter of them are too afraid to make any change, trapped by their fears and lack of self-confidence.[56] 'If the diver always thought of the shark, he would never lay hands on the pearl,' said Sa'di, a Persian poet from the thirteenth century. Fine words, but that shark can be constantly on our minds, preventing us from plunging into a different future.

We may have identified a range of careers, or 'possible selves', which offer the prospect of fulfilling work: perhaps starting a small business, retraining as a solicitor, or becoming a freelance translator. But how can we develop the courage to change – and make the right choices along the way? Taking those essential next steps into the unknown requires far more than pumping ourselves up with positive thinking. First, we need to understand the psychology of fear, and why the idea of changing profession can create such anxiety. Second, we must start testing our possible selves in reality by undertaking experimental projects such as 'radical sabbaticals', 'branching projects' and 'conversational research', which I will go on to discuss. Finally, we should explore the concept of 'flow', which is not only one of the three key components of fulfilling work – together with meaning and freedom – but which can help us choose effectively between the options.

It will gradually become clear that our greatest hope for overcoming our fear of change and finding a life-expanding career is to reject the traditional model of career change, which advises us to plan meticulously then take action, and replace it with the opposite strategy, which is to act now and reflect later. We must adopt Leonardo da Vinci's adventurous credo, 'experience will be my mistress'.

Why We Are Afraid of Change

Nearly everyone who contemplates changing career is deeply anxious about doing so. While there are a lucky few who possess the courage of mythical Greek heroes like Odysseus, most of us are haunted by fears that can prevent us from travelling in new directions. We worry that the job might not offer the satisfactions we had expected, or that we won't succeed in a new field, or that we are too old to change, or that we can't afford the financial risk with a big mortgage still to pay, or that we may be unable to return to our old job if our plan to become a puppeteer or perfumier doesn't work out.

Fear of failure is close to being a universal affliction. I have heard it expressed – in private – by everyone from burly army officers to millionaire CEOs, from government ministers to famous novelists. 'I tell very few people about my doubts – I'm outwardly confident but inside I'm not even sure I'm mediocre,' a prize-winning documentary maker told me. 'Can I really do it?' is a question carved into most of our souls.

It can be consoling to know that we are not alone in our uncertainties. When Anne Marie Graham decided, after twelve years, to leave her job as a project manager for a translation company and join a charity promoting foreign-language learning, she was anxious about succeeding in an area where she had little experience:

> Moving from something you know inside-out to something which you know nothing about is quite scary when you are over 30. There were times in that first year when I felt lost, convinced I was doing a rubbish job and was completely out of my depth. I would sit in meetings where everyone sounded so knowledgeable and I knew I was blagging it. Then one evening, as I shared my concerns over dinner, my partner pointed out that everyone else might be blagging it too. That suggestion started to lift the cloud of doubt in my own abilities. I also remembered that my old job was daunting at first too – it was just so long ago I had forgotten. It was a realization that made a huge difference to my confidence.

Yet even if we know that others share our fears, and are similarly riddled with doubts behind a carapace of outward self-confidence, we still need to understand why anxiety about career change looms so large in our lives. Why can't we just shake it off, send that resignation email and bound out of the door to do something new?

An answer lies in the peculiar attitude of human beings towards risk. In the 1970s psychologists Amos Tversky and Daniel Kahneman began a series of experiments that explored how we evaluate potential losses and gains, and discovered that we hate losing twice as much as we love winning, whether at the gaming table or when considering career change. According to Tversky, 'people are much more sensitive to negative than to positive stimuli . . . There are a few things that would make you feel better, but the number of things that would make you feel worse is unbounded'.[57] Evolutionary biologists have attempted to explain why we have this strong negative bias that means we focus much more on potential drawbacks than benefits. They speculate that it may be because early humans developed a high sensitivity to danger as a means of survival on the badlands of the African savannah: we are products of the primal terror experienced by our hominid ancestors. That hazy object in the distance could be a fruit-laden bush, but it might be a lion – best to steer well clear.

So when it comes to career change, we are psychologically disposed to magnify everything that could go wrong. Similarly, when thinking about whether a new job might suit us, we are more likely to highlight our personal weaknesses than our strengths. We find ourselves saying, 'I don't have the financial brain to run a social enterprise' more loudly than 'I'm great at generating creative ideas'. The result is that we tend to exhibit extreme caution, and remain in jobs that – at least in terms of fulfilment – are long past their sell-by date.[58]

'Without self-confidence we are as babes in the cradle,' wrote Virginia Woolf. She's right. The question, then, is how to let go of our fears, overcome our aversion to risk, and discover the courage we need to change.

Experimental Projects, or How to Have Thirty Jobs in One Year

Laura van Bouchout finally decided that she needed some professional advice. In her late twenties, and having already had five jobs – most of which involved organizing cultural events – she felt at a dead end, unable to find a career she loved. Luckily, in Belgium, where she lives, anybody who has worked for over twelve months is entitled to free sessions with a career coach. She booked an appointment, and after taking a standard personality test and being asked some probing questions, was told that she had been doing the wrong jobs for her personality. Now came the hard part: working out exactly what the right job might be. The coach told Laura to write down her dream careers, and the jobs of famous people she admired. But when Laura returned for the next session with a wildly long list covering several pages, the coach was as confused as she was. 'He didn't know where to start or what to advise me,' she recalls. 'I left the counselling sessions without an answer, but after moaning about it to my friends for a couple of months, I thought I'd take a risk and conduct an experiment.' This is what she did:

> I decided to try out thirty different jobs in the year leading up to my thirtieth birthday, dedicating the whole year to my career struggle. So I'm working as a part-time programmer of music events to pay the bills, and in my leisure time I contact people who I think have dream jobs or interesting careers and ask if I can follow them or work with them for at least three days. So far I've 'been' a fashion photographer, a bed-and-breakfast review writer, a creative director at an advertising agency, an owner of a cat hotel, a member of the European parliament, a director of a recycling centre and a manager of a youth hostel.
>
> The more jobs I try, the more I realize it's not a rational process of listing criteria and finding a job that matches them. It's a bit like dating. When I was single I had a mental list of qualities I thought my boyfriend should have. But some guys who met all the criteria on my list did nothing for me. And at one point you find someone who doesn't meet half your checklist but blows you away. I think that's what you have to look for in a job. I found it when following the advertising director; I was totally swept off my feet even though working in an advertising agency doesn't nearly match my ideals. So maybe it's not about thinking and planning, but about doing lots of job dating, trying things out until you feel a spark.

During the course of her thirty-job odyssey, Laura stumbled upon the most significant insight to have emerged in the last three decades of research into career change: act first, and reflect later.

Ever since Frank Parsons set up his Vocation Bureau in Boston over a century ago, the conventional wisdom for finding a new career has been to 'plan then implement'. This model typically starts with a deep internal exploration, drawing up lists of your personal strengths and weaknesses, and your skills, interests and ambitions, perhaps with the help of a psychometric test or a career advisor. This is followed by thorough research into various industries and professions to find out which best match your preferences and abilities. Having made a final decision, you create an action plan, and start sending out your CV and making job applications.

The problem with the 'plan then implement' model is simple: it rarely works. What generally happens is that we find ourselves in new jobs that don't suit us, because we haven't had any experience of what they are like in reality. As Laura would put it, the job matches our checklist, but we fail to fall in love. Alternatively, we spend so much time trying to work out what the perfect career would be, ceaselessly researching or getting lost in confused thoughts about the best option, that we end up doing nothing, overwhelmed by fears and procrastination, trapped by the paradox of choice I discussed earlier.

The art of career change requires turning the conventional approach on its head. We should wean ourselves off the rational-planning mentality and replace it by a philosophy of 'act first, reflect later'. Ruminating in an armchair or poring through files at a career centre is not what we need. We must enter a more playful and experimental way of being, where we *do then think*, not *think then do*.

The most recent research shows that successful change requires a substantial dose of experiential learning. Just like we can't learn carpentry from a book, we can't shift careers without taking practical action. First we should identify a range of 'possible selves' – careers that we believe might offer us purpose and meaning (the previous chapter should have helped with this). Then, like Laura, we have to trial them in reality by undertaking experimental projects. Following a period of job dating, we will be in a position to make better and more concrete decisions. As Herminia Ibarra argues:

> By far the biggest mistake people make when trying to change careers is to delay taking the first step until they have settled on a destination . . . The only way to create change is to put our possible identities into practice, working and crafting them until they are sufficiently grounded in experience to guide more decisive steps . . . We learn who we are by testing reality, not by looking inside . . . Reflection best comes later, when we have some momentum and when there is something new to reflect on.[59]

Experimental projects take three main forms, which I will address in descending order of personal challenge: radical sabbaticals, branching projects and conversational research. They are designed to suit different kinds of people, with different career ambitions, at different stages of their journey. All of them, though, can help pinpoint which of our possible selves offers the greatest prospect for fulfilment.

We have already encountered the first and most demanding form, the radical sabbatical. This was Laura van Bouchout's approach, and involves granting yourself a dedicated period for action-based projects, such as shadowing or accompanying people in their work, or volunteering in an appealing organization. Laura gave herself the unusual birthday present of a whole year to flirt with thirty possible future selves. She had no clear destination, just a basketful of ideas, and made space in her life by working part-time to support herself, which left her plenty of time for experiential adventuring. But you might equally pursue a radical sabbatical – what I also think of as a 'job holiday' – by taking a few months of unpaid leave, or using a couple of weeks of your annual vacation. In fact, I think it would be a good idea if we all spent at least one week every year trying out a different career, even if we believe we are happy in our existing job. We may not even realize that we are unfulfilled until we immerse ourselves in an alternative world. Who knows – running a cat hotel might turn out to be unexpectedly rewarding.

A second and more common form of experimental project is the branching project, or what Ibarra calls a 'temporary assignment'. One of the most pervasive myths of career change is the belief that it requires a drastic shift to a completely new life, where we march into work on Monday morning and hand in our resignation, then boldly step into the unknown. That would put off almost anybody. But with branching projects, such a risky strategy is not necessary, because they are designed as short experiments pursued around the edge of our existing career, through which we test out our possible selves. Apart from options such as work shadowing or volunteering, we could do a training course that gives us a taste of a different career, or try out an initial, scaled-down version of a prospective job.

As an example of the latter, imagine that you felt stuck in your job as a literary agent and were thinking of becoming a yoga teacher. What should you do? Stop thinking about it and get into action by starting to teach yoga in your spare time, perhaps on a weekday evening or on the weekend, to discover whether it really does provide that spark of radical aliveness that you hoped for. If it does, you can gradually increase your teaching commitments until you feel confident about leaving your old career behind you.

In effect, you will have taken a number of small and relatively unrisky steps, but which have led to big results. With each step you take the more confident you will feel, making the journey easier as you go along, and circumventing your inbuilt evolutionary aversion to risk. You will no longer wonder whether you might enjoy being a yoga instructor: after just a few classes you will have a pretty good sense of whether it is right for you, since there is no better way of learning than direct experience. And if it doesn't feel right, then you can start on another branching project to test a different possible self, perhaps spending a month of Saturdays helping a friend who has an online vintage-clothing store. It may take some time to work your way through several selves, but there is compelling evidence that this is a necessary part of the process of successful change. 'We short-circuit it at our own peril,' warns Ibarra.[60]

I can personally endorse the idea of branching projects, having pursued one which took my career in a radically new direction. After several years as the project director at a small foundation, I had a yearning to leave and start running my own workshops on the art of living. But I was worried about the financial risks of doing so, and was equally anxious about whether they would be a success. After months of talking about it to my partner – should I stay or should I go? – she suggested I stop talking, take out my diary and choose a date for my first workshop. That's exactly what I did. I sent out an email to friends and recruited ten guinea pigs. Unable to find a venue, I ran the first session in my kitchen one Saturday, on how to rethink our attitudes to love and time. After a few more weekend courses around the kitchen table – and while still working at the foundation – I approached the QI Club in Oxford and asked if they would host an evening class on the art of living as part of their public events programme. It soon became a regular gig, the classes grew in popularity, and within a few months I felt assured enough to leave my day job, having overcome my primal fear of failure.

A final form of experimental project is conversational research. Perhaps less daunting than a radical sabbatical or a branching project, it can be just as effective. It simply requires talking to people from different walks of life who are engaged in the types of work you might imagine doing. That may strike you as an obvious strategy. But it is worth thinking about why conversation is such a vital component of almost any successful career change.

One of the greatest obstacles to change is that we get trapped by the strictures of our social circle and peers. If you are a lawyer, and spend most of your time with other lawyers or professionals, this is likely to condition your ideals and aspirations: you may feel that you need to have a relatively high salary, or a nice house and luxurious holidays, and that working sixty hours a week is quite normal. In other words, our social milieu strongly determines what the German sociologist Karl Mannheim called our *Weltanschauung* or 'worldview' – our underlying mental frame of reference and belief system. The problem is that we may rarely interact with those who see the world very differently. As Tolstoy noted, most people 'instinctively keep to the circle of those people who share their views of life and their own place in it'. When was the last time you spent an afternoon with a bee keeper or a shamanic healer?

The result is that our existing priorities and values are constantly reinforced. You might dream of leaving the law to become a teacher in a Steiner school, but you will probably conclude that it is a whimsical, unrealistic idea – and so will most of your friends. As I know from my own experience, our worldview is a psychological straitjacket that restricts us from pursuing new possibilities. When I was finishing university, the only job options I could think of were working in investment banking, joining the civil service or becoming a journalist. Why was my imagination so extraordinarily narrow? Because those were the standard career paths considered by most of my college peers. Like almost everyone else, I followed the crowd. (In case you are interested, I crashed out of my banking interviews because I kept talking about my bonsai-tree collection rather than currency trading; I failed the civil service exams; and so I became a journalist – but not for long.)

One of the best ways to escape the confines of our worldview is to shift our peer group and talk to people whose work experiences and daily lives are very different from our own. If you really want to ditch law, it might be wise to spend less time with your lawyer friends, good company though they may be. More specifically, you can learn an enormous amount by having conversations with people who have made career changes that match where you hope to be heading. If you really are drawn to teaching at a Steiner school, can you find a Steiner teacher who was once a lawyer or doctor, and take them out to lunch? If you are a jaded academic hoping to become a garden designer, you should do everything you can to find a fellow scholar who has made this same move, or some other radical change.

Conversational research is also a particularly good strategy for making discoveries about careers that are difficult to test out in branching projects. Imagine you are a yoga instructor who is considering becoming a literary agent. Unlike experimenting with teaching yoga, it's difficult to trial yourself as a literary agent: you can't exactly set up a mini agency in your spare time and try attracting a few client authors to see if you like it. A much more viable starting place is using every contact you have to arrange a meeting with a literary agent, where you can discuss the ups and downs of their everyday working life – and find out whether publishing lunches really are as long as is commonly believed.

Such conversations bring us closer to understanding the realities of career change, with all its pleasures and pains. Hearing first-hand stories from people, and asking them the questions that intrigue or concern us, is worth far more than reading about a profession in a glossy career guide, and can give us a vivid yet nuanced picture of a different life we might aspire to. Furthermore, studies of career change consistently show that most people find new jobs through personal contacts rather than official channels, and that shifting career requires developing new social networks.[61] Conversational research creates openings in both these realms.

Andy Bell knows just how powerful conversation can be. After dropping out of school at 16, he was offered work in a travel agency in a small English town, as part of a state-sponsored youth-training scheme. He hated it: they made him cut his punk hairdo and take out his earrings. Andy left after a couple of months and found a job on a building site. And that's where his conversational world exploded into life:

> I met some wonderful people who told me loads of stories about travelling. It was a real education. The crew were all

> hippies who had travelled and become tradespeople – carpenters, plasterers, roofers, bricklayers. It was great fun, getting up in the morning and going to work and just having conversations with them. I found them inspiring partly because they were from a different social background than me – they were ordinary people, working people, they weren't from pampered backgrounds or spoilt brats. Hearing all these fantastic stories about driving to India, being at death's door with malaria, going to Morocco and staying with the Berber people. It all sounded so appealing – the only place I'd been abroad was when I went camping for two weeks in Spain.
>
> It definitely influenced my life. My aspirations then were to save up some money and go travelling, which is what I did for the next six years. I went to work in Greece for about two years, doing farm work, digging graves, unloading the frozen-fish trucks, laying irrigation pipes. I did it in Israel too: digging graves, furniture removal, delivering tiles. I ended up in New Zealand, becoming a full-time farmhand. I've probably done twenty or thirty jobs in my life.

Eventually Andy returned to England and started a small business as an organic farmer, running a weekly vegetable-box scheme delivering his produce direct to people's homes. As he himself admits, he wouldn't be where he is today without those conversations on the building site, which did so much to broaden his imagination and shift his worldview.

So what will it be? A radical sabbatical, a branching project, or a conversational exploration? The moment has come to lay this book aside and take action. My advice at this point is as follows:

- *Brainstorm three possible selves, then think of three ways you could 'act now, and reflect later' to test each of these selves. Give yourself half an hour right now and get started. Phone an organization that interests you and ask if they take on volunteers. Register a domain name for a business idea you have. Order a prospectus for a training course you could take. Email a wide-achiever friend and ask if you could meet to discuss how they manage it.*

Even taking small steps such as these can give you an uplifting sense that you are making change and be catalysts for re-forging your future. No time? Too tired? Worried nobody will want to speak with you? Then allow Goethe to lead the way. He understood the wisdom of acting now, reflecting later:

> Then indecision brings its own delays,
> And days are lost lamenting o'er lost days.
> Are you in earnest? Seize this very minute;
> What you can do, or dream you can, begin it;
> Boldness has genius, power and magic in it.

I Flow, Therefore I Am

The quest to find fulfilling work begins with acting, but is resolved by reflecting. Because even when we have tested a selection of our possible selves, we still need to judge which is the best option (or combination of options, for wide achievers). How can we know which career is right for us at this time in our lives? We ought to ask ourselves some basic questions about the worlds of work we've dipped into through branching projects or other experiments:

- *How were the careers you explored different from what you had expected?*
- *Which kind of work did you find yourself talking to people about afterwards with most enthusiasm?*
- *Which best provides the kinds of meaning you're looking for in a career?*

The last question is vital, because meaning is the ballast of a fulfilling career. But we should recognize that meaning is not sufficient for human fulfilment: you might use your talents as a sculptor, but nevertheless feel lonely much of the time as you hack away at the stone. Most of us also want to enjoy our jobs on a day-to-day basis. That prompts another question about the jobs you tried:

- *Which gave you the best 'flow' experience?*

Flow has the potential to provide this sense of daily enjoyment. Never heard of it? Don't worry. Let me explain what this mysterious elixir of flow is, and how exactly it can help us choose a career.

The concept of flow dates from the 1970s, when it was first developed by the Hungarian-American psychologist Mihaly Csikszentmihalyi (and you thought Krznaric was difficult to pronounce). It is now widely accepted as one of the most fundamental indicators of 'life satisfaction' or 'happiness'. A flow experience is one in which we are completely and unselfconsciously absorbed in whatever we are doing, whether it is scaling a rock face, playing the piano, doing pilates, giving a conference presentation, or conducting a surgical operation. As Csikszentmihalyi puts it, we are 'so involved in an activity that nothing else seems to matter'. When this happens, we are 'in flow', a state that athletes often describe as being 'in the zone'. He says that we enjoy such activities because they are 'autotelic', or intrinsically motivating: the action is valuable in itself, not a means to an end. In a typical flow experience, we feel totally engaged in the present, and future and past tend to fade away – almost as if we were doing Buddhist meditation. In his renowned study of surgeons, Csikszentmihalyi found that when performing operations, 80 per cent of them lose track of time or feel that it passes much faster than usual. They're in the zone.[62]

One of the curious characteristics of flow, according to Csikszentmihalyi, is that it is not limited to 'high-end' professions like being a surgeon, but can equally be experienced by butchers, welders or farm workers. He would certainly recognize the presence of flow in the following scene from Tolstoy's *Anna Karenina*, when the shy aristocrat Levin joins the peasants on his country estate in a day of scything:

> Swath followed swath. They mowed long rows and short rows, good grass and poor grass. Levin lost all count of time and had no idea whether it was late or early. A change began to overcome his work which gave him intense satisfaction. There were moments when he forgot what he was doing, he moved without effort . . . The longer Levin mowed, the oftener he experienced those moments of oblivion when it was not his arms which swung the scythe but the scythe

> seemed to mow of itself . . . These were the most blessed moments.

Perhaps an excessively romantic portrayal of life as a serf in nineteenth-century Russia, yet it is the kind of existential state that most of us have experienced. What kinds of activities typically give us flow? It most commonly occurs when we are using our skills to do a task that is challenging, but not so hard that we fear failing. That's why surgeons get a lot of it: the operations they perform are difficult and require immense concentration, but they are sufficiently trained that they feel confident of success. Flow is also enhanced when we are being creative and learning new skills, when we can see the immediate impact of our actions, and when we have clearly defined goals.[63] I am generally in flow while writing a chapter like this one, but not when answering administrative emails at the end of the day.

The implication of the flow theory is that we should aspire to be working in a career that offers us a high flow content. But this is the point at which it gets controversial. Csikszentmihalyi and many of his followers claim that almost any job can be altered so that 'its conditions are more conducive to flow'.[64] Even an apparently mundane job such as being a supermarket cashier, he says, can be approached in a way that makes it brimming with flow. So we may not need to change our career at all if we are feeling miserable in it: we just need to give ourselves more challenging tasks, or focus on the creative aspects of the work.

The problem is that the majority of jobs cannot be magically transformed to provide better flow experience. It might be possible if you are a fashion photographer, by deciding to shoot in more demanding

Jackson Pollock painting. What gives you flow experience?

locations or by playing around with new lighting techniques. But if you are deeply unhappy working as an IT project manager, you are unlikely to be able to recalibrate your daily tasks so they give you all the challenge, creativity and purpose you need to experience flow. Most workers, especially those in bureaucratic organizations or who do repetitive tasks, just don't have that much scope to alter their own jobs. I have consistently found that people who feel unfulfilled in their jobs are unable to adjust them sufficiently so that they can squeeze substantially more flow from them.

So instead of trying to *create* flow in our existing job, I believe that a more sensible path to pursue is to *find* work that gives us flow. Where can you discover that secret list of high-flow careers? It would be rash of me to offer one, because each of us experiences our work differently, depending on our skills, creative resources, fears and foibles. Which is precisely why it is so important to conduct branching projects: the best way to discover whether a career has high flow potential for you is to have a go at doing it. You can then choose between the options on the basis of which is most likely to put you in the zone.

The idea of flow can help us make career decisions in two other ways. First, through conversation. When talking to people whose jobs interest you, don't just ask vague questions such as 'What's it like being a taxidermist?'; ask them about flow – how often do they have that sense they are in the zone, and what precisely are they most likely to be doing when this occurs? A second strategy is to become a detective of flow in your own life by creating a Flow Diary. Spend a month keeping a daily note of the kinds of activities that give you flow – whether it is writing a tricky report at work, or cooking a Sunday lunch for a dozen people. You can then use this knowledge to help identify potentially fulfilling careers.

We must set our sights on finding a career that allows us to sing out to the world: I flow, therefore I am. But we should nevertheless beware becoming a flow junkie. Flow isn't everything. Necessary, yes. But sufficient on its own, no. We could be doing those challenging and creative flow tasks, yet still not find our work ultimately rewarding, because it does not embody our values or offer any of the other profound forms of meaning explored earlier. I used to experience flow when writing academic articles and lecturing, but I still didn't want to work as a university professor. What we need is both flow *and* meaning. Yet even this heady combination is not enough for the deepest forms of fulfilment. There is one more element we must consider, which is whether a job can offer us the liberating gift of freedom.

5. The Longing for Freedom

A Manifesto of Human Aspiration

In his book *Good Work*, the visionary economic thinker E.F. Schumacher lyrically describes the 'longing for freedom' that has become so widespread in Western society. This desire, he says, encapsulates a range of liberating ideas:

> I don't want to join the rat race.
> Not be enslaved by machines, bureaucracies, boredom, ugliness.
> I don't want to be a moron, robot, commuter.
> I don't want to become a fragment of a person.
>
> I want to do my own thing.
> I want to live (relatively) simply.
> I want to deal with people, not masks.
> People matter. Nature matters. Beauty matters. Wholeness matters.
> I want to be able to *care*.[65]

This poetic manifesto of human aspiration, written in the 1970s, is one that is likely to resonate with many people today who feel unfulfilled by their jobs. They may be suffering from chronic overwork

– one of the major causes of job dissatisfaction in the West – and typically arrive home exhausted after a stressful day and long commute, too tired to pursue their hobbies, go out with friends, or give their energies to family life.[66] They may enjoy aspects of their job, but dislike being told what to do all the time by haranguing bosses. They don't want their weekends to be constantly invaded by text messages and emails from the office. They talk about 'the rat race' or being a 'wage slave' or not having enough 'work–life balance'. They dream of more free time, more autonomy, more space in their lives for their relationships and to be themselves.

Not everybody feels these kinds of strictures: there are plenty of people who revel in hard work and long hours, passionately devoting themselves to careers they love. But if you have ever felt overburdened by work, and wished for more freedom and independence to live your life the way you want to, it may be worth considering this simple question: How can we satisfy a desire for greater freedom? The answer, however, is far from simple, and requires addressing three dilemmas. First, whether we should opt for the security and stability of a salaried job or embrace self-employment and invent our own job. Second, whether we ought to wean ourselves off the hard-work ethic by abandoning the goal of finding fulfilling work, and instead seek work for a fulfilling life. Third, the question of how we can balance our career ambitions with the desire to have a family, since trying to do both can not only create emotional strains, but put immense pressure on the limited hours at our disposal.

While exploring these issues we will meet an anarchist, a Wall Street analyst and a beekeeper. They will help us to recognize the virtues of idleness, to challenge the ideology of 'having it all', and to understand how freedom can be combined with meaning and flow to offer the most profound form of career fulfilment.

The Anarchist Alternative, or How to Invent Your Own Job

'Those who would give up essential liberty, to purchase a little temporary safety,' wrote Benjamin Franklin, 'deserve neither liberty nor safety.' Was he right? In deciding which career to pursue, we need to find a way to balance our twin desires for security and freedom. Most of us want some kind of stability in our working lives, especially in uncertain economic times: we need a regular income to repay the mortgage or hefty student loans, to support our children, and to ensure we have a pension for old age. At a deeper psychological level, from the moment the umbilical cord is cut and we are cast out into the loneliness of our individuality, we are in search of emotional and material security.[67] Although we may find it in a loving marriage or membership of a community, it can also be found in the workplace through a steady job that not only gives us a guaranteed pay check at the end of the month, but can also provide a network of friendships, a sense of identity and a feeling that we are valued. It was this overwhelming desire for security – rooted in a turbulent wartime childhood – that kept my father working at IBM for half a century.

While security may be at the foundation of our hierarchy of needs, human beings are equally driven by the quest for individual freedom. Throughout history, from the slave revolts under the Romans to the campaigns against apartheid in South Africa, social and political struggles have been fired by the yearning to escape oppression and enjoy personal liberty. This history is echoed in our attitude towards work. For decades, industrial psychologists have observed that job satisfaction is directly related to 'span of autonomy', meaning the amount of each day during which workers feel free to make their own decisions.[68] In nearly every class I teach, there are people whose dream is to enjoy more autonomy by leaving their jobs in large organizations and working for themselves, perhaps opening a small cafe or going freelance.

Their longing for freedom is perfectly understandable, according to Colin Ward, one of the most distinguished anarchist thinkers of the twentieth century. In his classic primer, *Anarchy in Action*, he asks the fascinating question of why a person will happily pick up a shovel and work in their garden after returning from a hard day at the factory or office:

> He enjoys going home and digging in his garden because there he is free from foremen, managers and bosses. He is free from the monotony and slavery of doing the same thing day in day out, and is in control of the whole job from start to finish. He is free to decide for himself how and when to set about it. He is responsible to himself and not to somebody else. He is working because he wants to and not because he has to. He is doing his own thing. He is his own man.
>
> The desire to 'be your own boss' is very common indeed. Think of all the people whose secret dream or cherished ambition is to run a small-holding or a little shop or to set up in trade on their own account, even though it may mean

> working night and day with little prospect of solvency. Few of them are such optimists as to think they will make a fortune that way. What they want above all is the sense of independence and of controlling their own destinies.[69]

Ward offers a compelling vision of fulfilling work. Wouldn't you rather have that sense of independence and free choice than spend eight hours each day servicing the needs of your employer, whose bottom line is more likely to be quarterly profits than your personal wellbeing? It is also a realistic vision, recognizing that the freedom of self-employment may require hard graft. Ward belongs to an anarchist tradition that is not the media stereotype of black-masked youths throwing bottles at the police, but one reaching back to the eighteenth-century philosopher William Godwin, which argues that anarchism is about expanding the space in society for individual freedom and social cooperation, outside the realm of corporate business and authoritarian government institutions. His workplace heroes are precisely those people who start up their own cafe, or who work in a health-food cooperative where the employees jointly own the business. So if you've ever felt frustration at your lack of autonomy, and crave the independence of working for yourself, then you might have an anarchist lurking within you.

It may, however, be possible to feel freedom working in a big organization, especially if you are able to choose your daily tasks and targets, and are offered benefits such as flexitime. Many firms pride themselves on how much autonomy they give their workers. When I was an academic, I may have been employed by a large bureaucratic institution, but I also enjoyed considerable freedom to decide how and when I worked: I did my first two hours of work while lying in bed at home, before arriving at my department at eleven in the morning. Nobody seemed to mind, as long as I kept publishing research papers and performed my teaching duties.

But if you seek genuine autonomy, you are much more likely to find it by joining the 20 per cent of Europeans and North Americans who are self-employed. And the chances are that it will be good for you. 'Working for yourself makes you happy,' according to the UK's Work Foundation: 47 per cent of self-employed people say they are 'very satisfied' with their jobs, compared to only 17 per cent of those in regular employment.[70]

Fiona Robyn will tell you that such statistics mask a far more complex and challenging reality. After years working in customer services for a major corporation, she retrained as a counsellor to enjoy the liberation of self-employment. When her therapy client list grew thin after moving to a diferent part of Britain to live with her husband, she decided to try earning a living from her greatest love, which was writing. So she set up Writing Our Way Home, a small business inspired by her commitment to Buddhism, which offers month-long online courses to a global community of people who want to use writing to increase their engagement with the world. Would she recommend self-employment?

> Being self-employed is wonderful and awful. There's no holiday or sick pay, no security. No development opportunities are offered to me unless I pay for them myself, and there's nobody to tell me I'm doing a good job or even notice how hard I'm working. Work easily bleeds into before breakfast,

> after dinner and weekends if I'm not careful. If things go wrong, there's no one else to blame or to discuss things with.
>
> Having said that, I wouldn't have it any other way. I love being able to manage my own diary, build relationships with the people I want to build relationships with, and know that I'm forging my own way through the world of work. I love knowing that what I'm doing is making a real difference to people – they tell me so.
>
> It's helpful to remember that the security I think I'm missing out on by not working for a corporation is non-existent anyway. People are made redundant, people get ill. There's never any guarantee that life will continue in the way we want it to for any length of time.

It is quite possible that Fiona's experience will convince you that self-employment – what some call a 'freestyle' career – is a crazy option. Who needs all that insecurity, stress and the prospect of no weekends? She could be right that ultimately nobody is safe in their job: the recent financial crisis has shown that we are all expendable when the markets demand it. Yet it may seem far too risky to forgo a regular wage during a recession or if you are anxious about whether your new independent career will be a success.

On the other hand, Fiona offers a profound insight into the value of freedom for the art of living. Almost everyone I've spoken to who has switched to self-employment has reached the same conclusion as Fiona: despite all the uncertainties, responsibilities and frustrations, they would still not give it up to return to being employed in a nine-to-five job. Once they have tasted freedom, it is almost impossible to turn back. That is a remarkable fact that should be a lesson to us all.

Fiona also provides an example of the most radical form of self-employment, which is to invent your own job – a bespoke career. This is an aspiration with origins in the Renaissance ideal of expressing individuality and uniqueness, but which has been more recently promoted by the management expert Charles Handy:

> For the first time in the human experience, we have a chance to shape our work to suit the way we live instead of our lives to fit our work . . . We would be mad to miss the chance.[71]

A bespoke career, sometimes described as a 'customized job', is one which you design yourself to suit your particular interests, talents and priorities. Typically they cannot be found in a standard career guide, such as Fiona's job of running online writing courses with a Buddhist twist. They also usually involve being self-employed, so you can decide exactly when and how you work. Inventing your own job is becoming increasingly common: there are people who earn their daily bread working as professional whistlers and travelling pizza chefs. Needless to say, these are not professions featured at any careers fair.

The internet has revolutionized the possibilities for custom-designed jobs, especially for those with a little entrepreneurial flair. I know of a woman who lives in a village in rural Mexico while teaching English as a foreign language to students in Italy and Japan. How does she do it? Using Skype, which allows her to have low-cost, face-to-face conversations with them. I find this technological advance extraordinary, having memories of teaching English to Spanish engineers in the mid-nineties, when I had to get up at five each morning and travel by bus to a remote industrial estate north of Madrid. Today you can also set up and launch a business for free in a single day by opening an account on eBay and offering a few homemade craft items for sale. Eventually you may become one of the estimated half a million people whose main income comes from selling on the site.[72] Niche products now have access to global markets: your online crossbow magazine can reach archery addicts from Beijing to Buenos Aires. Further opportunity has emerged from large companies and organizations farming out a huge portion of their work to freelance consultants, following years of downsizing. So you might be able to work from home for multiple employers, perhaps from several countries, and take a midday bubble bath without anybody knowing. This all leaves us with a question to ponder:

- *If you could create a bespoke career, what would it look like, and what branching projects would help transform it into reality?*

Inventing our own job might be too much of a gamble if we are running behind with mortgage repayments or bringing up a child alone. But if we wish to experience career fulfilment in its most sublime form, we ought to do everything we can to work in a way that suits who we are, with all our quirks and qualities. If we have a choice between security and freedom, I say choose freedom. This was a credo shared by the American hobo and explorer Chris McCandless, subject of the film and book *Into the Wild,* who died in the Alaskan wilderness in 1992:

> So many people live with unhappy circumstances and yet will not take the initiative to change their situation because they are conditioned to a life of security, conformity, and conservatism, all of which may appear to give one peace of mind, but in reality nothing is more damaging to the adventurous spirit within a man than a secure future.[73]

What if our ideal of freedom is not feeling free and independent *within* our job, but feeling free *from* our job? As we are about to see, that may require weaning ourselves off the work ethic, and developing a philosophy of idleness.

Weaning Yourself Off the Work Ethic

'All work is a form of voluntary enslavement.' Karl Marx? No, James Lam, an English-Chinese IT analyst. He works for a software company and has spent the last ten years in a series of IT posts. The pay is good but the hours are long and the stress is high. In one job he was regularly woken by his BlackBerry at two in the morning to fix urgent software problems. 'When I was 15, I was thinking of going on the road, leading a bohemian life like Jack Kerouac,' James told me. All these years he has retained his dream of greater freedom.

Why is it that so many people, like James, find themselves working too hard and too much in jobs they don't particularly enjoy? It may be that they consider it a price worth paying for a position that offers them an attractive financial package – the classic Faustian bargain of the modern workplace. Sociologists might alternatively suggest they are the unlucky inheritors of the Protestant work ethic, an ideology that emerged in seventeenth-century Europe, promoting the belief that hard work was good for you and would bring you closer to God. The legacy today is that we feel guilty if we are not putting in long days with our nose to the grindstone.

A third possibility is that they have succumbed to the current epidemic of work addiction. Over one million Britons say they are workaholics and voluntarily do extra hours. In Japan, 10 per cent of male deaths are job-related; they even have a special word for it, *karōshi*, death by overwork.[74] Those who end up as addicts tend to be initially lured by the benefits of working hard, such as the satisfactions of being a perfectionist, or the kudos of being last to leave the office. Eventually, however, their work obsession gets out of control. According to psychotherapist Bryan Robinson, we should be asking ourselves questions like 'Do I find myself doing two or three things at once, such as eating lunch and writing a memo?' and 'Do I put more time and energy into my work than into my relationships with loved ones and friends?' Answering yes could mean we are sliding into addiction, especially if we are regularly putting in a lot of 'voluntary hours' beyond official duties.[75] Of course, working a twelve-hour day does not necessarily mean we are workaholics: it might be a reflection of the fact that we have found a stimulating and absorbing vocation.

Assuming, however, that we are feeling overworked – whether we consider ourselves addicts or not – what might be the cure? To work less, obviously. Not particularly helpful advice, I'll admit. To make sense of it, we need to think about what it would take to wean ourselves off the work ethic, and what the implications might be for finding a job we love, as well as for our pockets. In the end, we may decide to shift our priorities: instead of thinking that the goal must be to find fulfilling work, our ambition could be to seek work for a fulfilling life.

The philosopher Bertrand Russell can help us explore the issues. In his scintillating 1932 essay 'In Praise of Idleness', Russell shocked the establishment by arguing that 'there is far too much work done in the world' and that 'immense harm is caused by the belief that work is virtuous'. He saw no good reason why people should be sweating away producing so many consumer goods that added little to quality of life. Like many progressive thinkers of his era, including the economist John Maynard Keynes, he was convinced that economic growth and technological advances had made it possible for most people in wealthy countries to enjoy a decent standard of living by working no more than four hours a day. Russell also thought we should recognize the virtues of leisure. By 'leisure' he didn't mean passive pastimes, but rather activities that could expand our human potential:

> In a world where no one is compelled to work more than four hours a day, every person possessed of scientific curiosity will be able to indulge it, and every painter will be able to paint without starving, however excellent his pictures may be . . . There will be happiness and joy of life, instead of frayed nerves, weariness and dyspepsia.[76]

If a four-hour day seems a little too ambitious, we might more realistically consider the possible benefits – and costs – of shifting to a four-day week, a popular aspiration since the 1970s, and one that

The philosopher Bertrand Russell (sitting on the right) believed we should all work a four-hour day. He used his 'leisure time' to co-found Britain's Campaign for Nuclear Disarmament.

employers are increasingly willing to accept. Or at the very least, imagine reducing your time at work by just one hour a day. Clearly, you would be left with more time for family and friends, which is exactly what 70 per cent of people say that excessive work is depriving them of.[77] Do you think your children would prefer to play with you for an extra hour each evening, or that you regularly stay late at the office so you can earn enough to afford a bigger home? As one friend of mine put it, 'I think my kids would rather have more father than more garden.'

A second benefit is that it might provide, as Russell suggests, the freedom to pursue life-enhancing projects outside official working hours. Take the case of the American poet Wallace Stevens. By day he worked in an insurance company, eventually becoming vice-president of an established firm in Connecticut. But he was no workaholic: he returned home each evening to write verse, and was considered one of the great modernist poets of the early twentieth century. Stevens kept these two lives separate: he always felt something of an imposter in his day job; it was 'like playing a part', he wrote. He regarded poetry as his 'real work' – even if he wasn't paid for it – and never wanted to commercialize his art by becoming a 'professional' poet. After winning the Pulitzer Prize in 1955 he was offered a faculty position at Harvard that would have allowed him to write poetry for a living, but he turned it down to stay in his insurance job.

In effect, Stevens opted not to make his daytime career the main project of his life, but used it as a foundation to pursue his wider ambitions as a human being. That's what I mean by 'seeking work for a fulfilling life'. It's a common strategy for the art of living: you hold down a job that leaves you sufficient time and energy for a serious free-time pursuit such as playing the fiddle, doing landscape photography, or being a community activist.

Does this imply giving up on the possibility of having a fulfilling career? Not necessarily. For a start, a meaningful job need not be one that completely consumes your whole life. I was once lucky enough to have a wonderful job organizing 'conversation meals' between strangers, but by agreeing with my boss that I'd work from noon until six, I could spend my mornings writing a novel. Moreover, fulfilment remains possible if we are willing to break down the conceptual barrier between work and leisure. So-called 'leisure activities' may not offer us hard cash, but they can provide many of the other benefits of a fulfilling career if we pursue them with dedication. Through his poetry, Wallace Stevens was able to obtain social status, respect from fellow poets, and a sense that he was using his talents and following his calling. So let's not be so hung up on the traditional idea that a career necessarily involves earning money.

But we can't just forget about money. Indeed, anxiety about money is the major factor preventing most people from following Bertrand Russell's advice and reducing their working hours so they have enough time for creative idling. Just imagine you convinced your employer to let you work four days a week instead of five. Could you survive the 20 per cent drop in salary?

The most effective way to meet this challenge is to become an adherent of simple living, one of the fastest-growing religions of our post-industrial age. By doing so, you would be joining a venerable tradition of individuals who have voluntarily turned against materialism and consumerism in pursuit of a more meaningful – and cheaper – existence. Think of the nineteenth-century American naturalist

Henry David Thoreau, who spent two years conducting an experiment in self-sufficiency in the 1840s. Thoreau lived in a log cabin he built with his own hands for less than $30, and kept his costs down by growing most of his own food. Devoting himself to reading, writing and observing nature, he famously declared in *Walden*, 'a man is rich in proportion to the number of things he can afford to let alone'.

Someone who followed his example was Joe Dominguez, a founder of the modern simple-living movement in the United States and co-author of *Your Money or Your Life*, one of its most influential manifestos. The son of poor Cuban immigrants, in the 1960s Dominguez climbed out of the ghetto and into a job as a financial analyst on Wall Street. 'When I worked on Wall Street,' he said, 'I saw that most people were not making a living, they were making a dying. They would come home from work a little deader than when they started out in the morning. I was determined not to make the same mistake.'[78] So he came up with a plan. He saved every cent he could, living cheaply in Harlem, making his own furniture and buying second-hand clothes. By the age of thirty he had put away enough money to be able to survive, if he was careful, on the annual interest of $6,000 a year. He resigned his job, bought a camper van, and headed out west into a new life of frugal freedom.

Thoreau and Dominguez approached simple living as an extreme sport, and few people are ready to make such a radical change in lifestyle. But if you doubt that you could get by on even 20 per cent less than you currently earn, or think that it wouldn't be worth the material sacrifices involved, let me share with you one of the great secrets of the art of living. You've probably experienced the phenomenon whereby an increase in your salary fails to lead to any increase in your savings, because your spending mysteriously expands to fill the space of your available income. Well, the reverse also applies. When your income goes down from working less (or maybe from taking a salary cut to do a more fulfilling job), as a general rule your daily living expenses – on things like food, clothing and entertainment – will naturally contract to fit your new financial circumstances, and yet you will not feel any worse off. In fact, it is quite likely that you will feel life is better than ever, since you will be luxuriating in an abundance of that most precious commodity, time.

Don't believe me? When Sameera Khan left her job as a corporate lawyer in London and took up working on social enterprise projects and doing sporadic legal work on a freelance basis, she and her husband had to adjust to a significant reduction in their joint income. I asked her how they were managing.

> We are thousands of pounds a month down. How on earth did we used to spend that money? I am ashamed to say that I have no idea what I spent it on. When you take it away you can live fine. And my quality of life has improved. I'm at home more, I see more of my friends, my family. I cook nice evening meals whilst being frugal as I can shop in the greengrocers or farmer's market rather than having to shop in Sainsbury's. I can go to the fishmonger and buy locally caught fish that is cheaper because it's from our shores. I'm finally applying the 'waste not, want not' ethos of my parents' generation, but I really wish I'd had the sense to apply this when I was earning a full salary. I get so much pleasure in not spending money. I've also had time to take hula-hoop lessons

> and teach myself how to knit on YouTube. I'm being creative – I didn't even know I was creative!
>
> Sure, we've had to make changes, we've taken a long hard look at how we spent money and why we spent it. I guess before I just wasn't focused on what I needed versus what I wanted. We can't as easily go out to expensive restaurant meals with friends because it's harder for us to justify the cost. When I want to treat myself, I try to earn some extra money through selling things I no longer need on eBay – it's quite addictive. Overall, the whole experience has taught me to be incredibly more reflective, and to value everything I've got.

Making a transition towards simpler living requires embracing Picasso's philosophy: 'art is the elimination of the unnecessary'. One worthwhile experiment is to keep detailed accounts for a month of all your expenses, labelling each item as a 'need' or a 'want', and in the following month trying to halve the spending on your 'wants'. Did your quality of life plummet, or was it surprisingly liberating? Another option is to cultivate yourself as a connoisseur of flea markets and second-hand shops, and sign up to online communities such as Freecycle, where people give away unwanted consumer goods, from tricycles to sofas. At the same time, it is important to recognize that our jobs can actually cost us money: think how much you spend on what Joe Dominguez called your 'work uniform' (suits, dresses, shoes, bags), on commuting to the office, daily snacks, and on luxury vacations to help you recover from the stress. Should you really be paying so much to be in work?

Simple living also has more general applications to career change. If you decide to take a radical sabbatical like Laura van Bouchout, an ability to live relatively cheaply may extend the amount of time you can give to your work experiments. And a knowledge that you are able to live lightly could make it easier to shift to a job with less pay but more meaning.

In a culture obsessed with hard work and career success, it can be difficult to wean ourselves off the work ethic. And we may not want to if we are engrossed in a career that is making us feel fully alive. But if we do seek the advantages of a four-day week, and the space to nurture other parts of who we are, then we might be wise to put our hopes in the virtues of simple living, discovering beauty in the ideal that less truly is more.

While we may be able to find a gratifying job which also leaves us with an abundance of idle hours for enriching projects, what will happen to our prospects for career fulfilment when we take on the ultimate project of having a family?

How to Think About 'Having it All'

It is eight o'clock on a Wednesday morning and I'm arguing with my partner about who will stay home to look after our three-year-old twins, who are too ill to go to nursery today. She's an economist at a development-aid agency, busy writing a report on alternatives to economic growth, and trying to hold down a demanding professional job on just three days a week. I'm struggling to meet my deadline to finish a book on how to find fulfilling work, within the confines of my four-day week. We love our children, but are also both immersed in our careers. Neither of us really wants to make what we each think of as a 'sacrifice' to do an unscheduled day of childcare.

This kind of dilemma is typical for anybody trying to 'have it all' – to pursue a fulfilling career while also being a dedicated parent. Unless you are one of the lucky few who have grandparents on call or can afford expensive childminders, there can be just too many demands on our time, especially when children are below school age. The result is not only lack of sleep and lack of space for ourselves. Under so much pressure, relationships can crumble, career ambitions fall by the wayside, and freedom of choice disappear.

Despite these challenging realities, having it all has become a widespread aspiration in Western society, especially since the 1980s when the phrase was popularized and became associated with the ideal of the 'superwoman' who had well-adjusted children, a great marriage and a top-flight job. But is it really possible – for both women and men – to combine a thriving career with an enriching family life? The best way to approach this question is not to answer it directly, but to demystify it. I want to suggest four ways of rethinking the issue of how to have it all.

Don't think of it as your dilemma, it's society's dilemma

If you are finding it hard to have an enjoyable and successful career while also bringing up children, remember this: it's not your fault. The time strictures and emotional strains you face are in large part a consequence of social and cultural factors that make it extraordinarily difficult, particularly for women, to have it all. This is not your work crisis, it's society's crisis.

One aspect of the problem is that men's attitudes towards family life have not changed sufficiently to keep pace with women's emancipation. The French philosopher and feminist Simone de Beauvoir recognized this back in the 1940s. When discussing the significant increase of women entering the paid workforce during the early twentieth century, she pointed out that 'it is through gainful employment that woman has traversed most of the distance that separated her from the male; and nothing else can guarantee her liberty in practice'. Yet she saw that the majority 'do not escape from the traditional feminine world' of childcare and housework, even if they have a job.[79]

De Beauvoir highlighted what has become known as the 'double burden': women doing paid work often face a 'second shift' of domestic work when they get back home, since they tend to do a far greater proportion of the household tasks than men, from cooking the evening meal to getting up in the night to comfort a crying baby. No wonder Erica Jong declared that liberated women 'have won the right to be terminally exhausted'. A revealing recent study by psychologist Paula Nicolson showed that first-time mothers who believed the father would be an equal partner in infant care were almost always wrong in their prediction.[80] Soon after the baby arrived, the men tended to step back into the traditional breadwinner role, and were unwilling to give up their old social life to take on domestic responsibilities. And don't be fooled by all those magazine articles about superdads: stay-at-home dads may be on the rise, but in countries like Britain only one in twenty fathers is the primary carer.[81] We continue to live in cultures that typically expect women to take on most of the childcare, and that assume it is the mother, more than the father, who should be adjusting her career to have a family.

A second factor compounding the problem is that the way work is structured is out of kilter with the realities of raising children. For instance, even when fathers want to get involved in childcare, employment laws in many countries only grant them a few weeks of paternity leave. If only we all lived in Norway, where couples can choose how to divide their forty-six weeks of paid parental leave between them, with the result that 90 per cent of fathers take at least three months of paternity leave.[82] Some countries, though, are beginning to catch up: new legislation in the UK will allow fathers to take six months of leave. A further barrier is that in most countries employees are given around four weeks of annual holiday, yet school children are on holiday for some twelve weeks. How are parents supposed to close the gap without at least one of them putting their work in the background? Similarly, schools tend to finish two hours earlier than the office day, with only a minority of workers enjoying flexitime that allows them to leave early to pick up the kids. In such a crazy system, so desperately in need of reform, you should hardly blame yourself for your frustrations when trying to balance career ambitions and family obligations.

'Can women have it all?' is the wrong question

An underlying assumption in most books and news articles about how to have it all is that this is primarily an issue for and about women. It is standard practice to interview a variety of mothers, some of whom manage the superhuman feat of being both a corporate CEO and a domestic goddess, while others struggle with the challenge. What is the great secret of those who have it all? We might meet one human dynamo who gets up at five each morning and is a genius at time management, and another who is a brilliant multitasker, able to negotiate a deal before whipping up a gourmet meal. An implicit message is often that women who aren't able to shine in both their job and as mothers are somehow inadequate and haven't quite got what it takes. As superwoman commentator Shirley Conran made clear two decades ago, this message has had a real impact:

> I had noticed a growing anxiety and depression among ordinary women as the result of media propaganda about females who effortlessly organize a career (not a 'job'), home, husband, children and social life, while simultaneously retaining a twenty-four-hour perfect hairstyle and doing something esoteric, such as learning Japanese in their spare time.[83]

But what about the men? While women are put under the spotlight, the men in their lives are usually left standing quietly in the background. Yet we can't fully understand the possibilities for working mothers unless we know what the men around them are doing. In traditional two-parent households, the factor that might make it possible for a woman to maintain a demanding career while spending quality time with her children is the support of a husband who cooks half the meals and works part-time from home. Equally, what might make it impossible for some women is not any personal failing, but the fact that their husbands barely lift a finger to help with domestic chores.

Focusing on women while neglecting the role of men also reinforces the cultural norm that it is mothers, rather than fathers, who should be adjusting their lives to the complexities of managing both a career and a family, and making compromises where necessary. If we want to live in a more equal society, where both men and women can enjoy fulfilling careers, we need to challenge this bias. The dilemmas of having it all ought to be faced by both sexes, and be negotiated by them together. Iain King, for instance, knew that his wife 'wanted some mental stimulation beyond juggling nappy changes with meal planning', so they decided that he would give up his peacekeeping job in Afghanistan and become a full-time househusband caring for their son, enabling her to return to her diplomatic career. Men should not presume that they can automatically continue working as they always have done once they have children, just as women need not assume that they are the ones who have to put their careers on hold to manage the household economy. Instead of asking 'Can women have it all?', the real question should be 'How can parents support each other so they can *both* have some of it all?'

Having it all does not mean you must have it all at once

Across Europe and North America, the most common strategy for reconciling the demands of work and family is for one parent – usually the mother – to shift to working part-time while the children are small. Yet the strictures of doing so can turn the idea of career fulfilment into a fantasy. Is it really possible to flourish in your chosen profession on a three-day week? Unlike your colleagues, you may, for example, be unable to go that extra distance and stay late at the office, because the kids need to be picked up from nursery. Many part-timers end up worrying that while they aren't able to do their jobs well, neither are they giving enough time to their children. 'I feel like I'm being good at nothing,' admits a child psychologist who juggles consulting work with caring for her three-year-old son.

An alternative approach is to avoid the juggling act by adopting the philosophy that having it all does not mean you must have it all at the same time. This requires stepping back to take the long view. Imagine your life as a series of phases, each expressing a different dimension of who you are – something like Shakespeare's Seven Ages of Man. The idea is to have a fully committed career phase, where you throw yourself into work, then switch to a phase of dedicated parenting, and perhaps return to work again at a later stage. In effect, stretching your ambition to 'have it all' over an extended time span. In pursuit of this strategy, professional women frequently choose to put off motherhood until their late thirties, to give themselves sufficient years to experience a feeling of career achievement.[84]

Like all strategies, this one has its risks, as Helena Fosh can tell you. She traded in her top job in advertising, where she was in charge of several multi-million-dollar accounts, to have a family. 'But two children later, I was secretly envious of the women I knew who were still working,' she remembers. 'They seemed to have a sense of purpose I lacked – I didn't think my contribution to my family's and husband's life was valued.' Helena discovered how difficult it can be to make the identity transition from 'successful professional' to 'full-time parent', which is not helped by the fact that being a parent is unpaid and has no promotion prospects. Helena's eventual solution was to try to return to the workplace. But she found not only that her CV and skills were out of date, but that her extended career break had eroded her self-esteem: 'A huge challenge has been to overcome my feelings of inadequacy and loss of self-confidence.' So now she believes that 'leaving a professional career is the worst mistake that a woman can make; women should always try to keep a foot in the door, at any cost, while raising a family'.

Not everyone would agree with this. There are many people who thrive on full-time parenting and think about it as the most fulfilling career they could imagine. They approach bringing up their children as a vocation that provides their life with a sense of meaning and direction. Unlike their previous paid work, where they may have felt expendable, they commonly feel that as a parent they are irreplaceable, the only person who can be mother or father to their own child. This idea of acknowledging that childcare is a job in itself is one promoted by feminist economists such as Nancy Folbre, who point out the huge social contribution and economic value of unpaid work such as childcare and housework. In Britain, for example, the average value of unpaid work by a mother in the home is estimated to be worth £30,000 a year, yet it remains invisible in the national accounts.[85]

Brian Campbell, a Canadian father who had to give up a promising career as a scholar of Chinese poetry to bring up four boys himself after he split up with his partner, adopted the attitude that child-rearing was a worthwhile form of work, albeit unpaid. 'I approached single parenting as a job,' he told me, describing how he even home-schooled his children for a couple of years. Although he regrets losing his chance of an academic career, 'I discovered that raising my kids, imparting to them my values, my passion for learning, for problem-solving and supporting them in every way possible, was a sacrifice worth making.' The rewards of working as a parent lie not in money or status, but in human relationships.

Raising children is an opportunity to go in new career directions

There is more to the story of Brian Campbell. When his kids were little, he thought it would be interesting if they all developed their botanical minds by learning about the bees buzzing around their garden. Soon he was drawn to keeping bees himself to earn some money on the side. Fifteen years later, with his children almost all grown up, Brian now leases a small farm, has hives all over the city, and teaches courses on urban beekeeping. 'I enjoy bees and sharing my passion for them with others,' he says. 'It took me a while to realize that this has become a career, alongside being a stay-at-home dad. It definitely wasn't planned; it just evolved slowly out of a need to support myself and my family. I suppose jobs become careers when they take on a life of their own.'

A final way of rethinking the problem of balancing work and family is to recognize that raising children can create unexpected opportunities for taking your career in different directions. Like Brian, many parents develop new interests and skills that grow out of their engagement in family life, which often sends them into startlingly unfamiliar territory. Tom Burrough, who became a full-time father after losing his job in the advertising industry, was appalled by the second-rate baby food on offer for his infant. So he started up a small business producing gourmet meals for babies, like Moroccan lamb stew and cod-and-pea mornay, while caring for his daughter. Keira O'Mara, an enterprising mother who was made redundant from her marketing job while on maternity leave, told me how she was tired of getting disapproving stares when trying to feed her baby in public, and so she invented Mamascarf, a new kind of breastfeeding scarf, which is now sold in retail outlets across Britain.

Rather than being the end of our career, or an extended pause, becoming a parent can signal a fresh beginning. A radical new experience like having children might leave us utterly exhausted at the end of each day, but it can also free our minds, encourage our creativity, and stir us to experiment with the worker bee buzzing in our souls.

The Captive Slave

Michelangelo's sculpture *The Captive Slave*, seemingly half-finished, shows a figure attempting to free himself from the stone. Some art historians interpret it as a metaphysical vision of the soul endeavouring to escape from matter. Others consider it a metaphor for how we need to discover our true selves and destinies, which lie hidden within us, like a figure within a block of stone. For me, this work of art is about the struggle for freedom in everyday life.

How much should freedom matter to us? I am not saying that we should all become self-employed fire jugglers, for there are times in life when job security is essential. I don't believe we should all

Michelangelo's captive slave, struggling to free himself from the stone.

join the revolution of idleness, since there are some people who will thrive on committing their entire being to their work. And of course compromise is sometimes a necessary part of life, especially when it comes to balancing career ambitions with tending to our children.

Yet I also believe it is a worthy aspiration to try to break free from the stone, to liberate ourselves from the personal fears, social conventions and myths that might be holding us back from releasing our adventurous spirit. There are many ways to free that spirit, from inventing our own job to unchaining ourselves from the culture of overwork by living a simpler life with more space for pursuing our passions. In the affluent nations of the modern world, there is no need for most of us to be captive slaves, to 'be enslaved by machines, bureaucracies, boredom, ugliness', as Schumacher put it. We have the ability, the obligation, to escape the stone by carving out new possibilities in our lives.

- *What is the kind of freedom that you most desire for your working life?*

6. How to Grow a Vocation

The Prize of Soulful Work

'Without work, all life goes rotten, but when work is soulless, life stifles and dies,' wrote Albert Camus. Finding work with a soul has become one of the great aspirations of our age. While the 'grin and bear it' school of thought still has its followers, there is a growing movement of people in the Western world and beyond who are asking more of their jobs, who seek work that reflects who they are and makes them feel more human. Those who wish to join this movement, and be successful in their quest for a life-expanding career, need to consider two final questions.

In this book I've tried to distil the very essence of a fulfilling career, and discovered that there are three essential ingredients: meaning, flow and freedom. People who are fulfilled have some combination of them, while also being wary of an excessive allegiance to the desire for money or status. Yet even those with all three elements in their working lives can feel there is a greater prize, what we might think of as the Holy Grail of soulful work: a career that is not just fulfilling, but that additionally feels like a 'calling' or 'vocation'. This raises the first question: how can we discover our true vocation in life?

There is another unresolved issue, which concerns how we complete the task of turning our ideal of fulfilment into the reality of a new career. We now know the fundamentals of this process.

Once we have narrowed down the options to a range of jobs that express our multiple selves, we need to test them out with radical sabbaticals, branching projects and conversational research. We must adopt the revolutionary philosophy of 'act now, reflect later', and become what Leonardo da Vinci called a *discepolo di esperienza,* a disciple of experience.

Yet even if we have followed this experimental pathway and identified a potentially fulfilling career, we still may find ourselves frozen in indecision, because we are too afraid to take that final – and unavoidable – step into the unknown that allows us to break with our past and reinvent ourselves. Thus emerges the second question: how can we overcome this barrier to change?

To answer these two questions, we must travel first to a scientific laboratory in Paris, then to small island off the coast of Greece.

Marie Curie and the Meaning of Life

In the classes I teach, I regularly hear people lament that they are 'still searching for their vocation' or envying others who have 'found their ultimate calling'. What they seem to be looking for is a career that offers them an all-embracing sense of mission or purpose. Their search, however, is almost certain to be unsuccessful. Not because vocations do not exist. But because we have to realize that a vocation is not something we *find*, it's something we *grow* – and grow into. Before revealing the secret of how to grow one, we need to be clear about what a vocation really means, and why it matters.

It is common to think of a vocation as a career that you somehow feel you were 'meant to do'. I prefer a different definition, one closer to the historical origins of the concept: a vocation is a career that not only gives you fulfilment – meaning, flow, freedom – but that also has a definitive goal or clear purpose to strive for attached to it, which drives your life and motivates you to get up in the morning. The goal or purpose for a medical researcher might be to discover a cure for motor neurone disease; for an environmental activist it could be to promote the ideal of low-carbon living; for a painter, to break traditional conventions and replace them with a new vision of the objectives of art. You shouldn't worry at all if you don't feel you have a vocation. However, while they are relatively rare, with the right approach it is quite possible for a vocation to emerge in your life.

Amongst the most important discoveries in the history of Western thought is that having this kind of clear goal or purpose to pursue is one of the surest routes to a deeply satisfying life. In fact, if there is any answer to the question of the meaning of life, this is a major contender. Aristotle was the first thinker to recognize it explicitly, writing that every person should have 'some object for the good life to aim at . . . with reference to which he will then do all his acts, since not to have one's life organized in view of some end is a mark of much folly.'[86]

The idea of having a meaningful goal re-emerged in the sixteenth-century Protestant concept of a 'calling'. This was the belief that each of us should follow the preordained path or 'calling' determined for us by God: so a farmer should grow his crops to the best of his abilities, and a magistrate should dedicate himself completely to his profession. Doing so, wrote the theologian John Calvin in 1536, would cure us of the 'great restlessness' that we often feel, and prevent our lives from being 'topsy-turvy'.[87] Calvin's views reflected the rigid social hierarchies of his time – we should be satisfied with the career we were born into – so bad luck if you happened to be a serf. But underlying this was the goal of striving to do God's bidding on earth.

The German philosopher Friedrich Nietzsche similarly stressed the beneficial effects of having a mission to guide us: 'He who has a *why* to live for can bear with almost any *how*.' This thought found its way out of philosophy and into twentieth-century psychology. In the 1940s, the Austrian psychotherapist Victor Frankl suggested: 'What man actually needs is not some tension-less state but rather the striving and struggling for some goal worthy of him.' Each of us should pursue a 'concrete assignment', which is our 'specific vocation or mission in life'.[88] This long tradition of thought is today reflected in the writings of psychologist Mihaly Csikszentmihalyi, who believes that 'wherever it comes from, a unified purpose is what gives meaning to life'. What people require is 'a goal that like a magnetic field attracts their psychic energy, a goal upon which all lesser goals depend'.[89] Aristotle would have thoroughly approved.

Let's leave the theory for a moment and examine the realities of a working life driven by this kind of missionary purpose: the career of Marie Curie, whose overriding goal was to discover the secrets of radiation.

Born into a studious but impoverished family of Polish intellectuals in 1867, Marie Curie – then known as Manya Skłodowska – was a gifted student. She dreamed of studying medicine in Paris, but lack of funds prevented this, and she was condemned to working as a governess in rural Poland for five years, saving her pennies and reading maths and anatomy books alone deep into the night. Finally arriving in Paris in 1891, aged 24, she commenced her medical studies, and gradually found herself drawn to doing research in chemistry and physics, an interest she had partly inherited from her father.

It was the beginning of an extraordinarily intensive life of scientific endeavour that would last over forty years. Curie normally worked twelve to fourteen hours a day, continuing at home until two in the morning after returning from the lab. In 1897 she began her study of radiation, in collaboration with her husband Pierre, which led to the discovery of radium a year later. This was followed by four years working in a draughty old shed to further explore the properties of radium, and another new element she discovered, polonium. Her brilliance and dedication were rewarded with a Nobel Prize in Physics in 1903, and another in Chemistry in 1911. She became France's first female university professor, and one of the world's most famous scientists.

Curie was absolutely committed to her career. She lived an almost monastic lifestyle in her early years in Paris, surviving on nothing but buttered bread and tea for weeks at a time, which left her anaemic and regularly fainting from hunger. She shunned her growing fame, and had no interest in material comforts, preferring to live in a virtually unfurnished home: status and money mattered little to her. When a relative offered to buy her a wedding dress, she insisted that 'if you are going to be kind enough to give me one, please let it be practical and dark, so that I can put it on afterwards to go to the laboratory'.[90] Before her death in 1934, aged 67, she summed up her philosophy of work. 'Life is not easy for any of us,' she said. 'But what of that? We must have perseverance and above all confidence in ourselves. We must believe that we are gifted for something, and that this thing, at whatever cost, must be attained.'[91]

What conclusions can we draw from Marie Curie's career? Certainly it had all the qualities of a vocation. Her work offered the fundamental elements of meaning: it used her intellectual talents, embodied her great passion for science, and allowed her to feel she was making a difference – especially in the potential uses of radiation therapy for cancer treatment. But she also had that Aristotelian sense of purpose, embodied in her goal, or 'concrete assignment', to make discoveries about the nature of radiation.

A more important point concerns where that goal actually came from. What everyone in the career doldrums really wants to know is: 'How can I find a vocation?' And the answer that emerges from Marie Curie's experience is that vocations are grown, and grown into, rather than found.

There is a widespread – and mistaken – assumption that a vocation usually comes to people in a flash of enlightenment or moment of epiphany. We're lying in bed and suddenly we know exactly what we're supposed to do with our life. It's as if the voice of God has called to us: 'Go forth and write Chinese-cookery books!' Alternatively we put ourselves through a process of intense self-reflection which, at some point, is supposed to give us a blinding insight into our future: 'My task in life is to set up an otter sanctuary!' It's an enticing thought, which, in effect, takes the responsibility away from us: someone or something will tell us what to do with our lives.

But Marie Curie never had such a miraculous moment of insight, when she knew that she must dedicate her working life to researching the properties of radioactive materials. What really occurred was that this goal quietly crept up on her during years of sustained scientific research. After an initial desire to become a doctor like her elder

Marie Curie didn't find her vocation. She grew it.

sister, she did research on the magnetization of tempered steel. Only at the age of 30 did she begin studying uranium rays for her doctoral thesis, building on recent work done by Henri Becquerel. Following her discovery of radium, several more years of experiments were required to prove its existence to an incredulous scientific establishment.[92] Her obsession grew in stages, without any Tannoy announcement from the heavens that issued her a calling. That's the way it typically happens: although people occasionally have those explosive epiphanies, more commonly a vocation crystallizes slowly, almost without us realizing it.[93]

So there is no great mystery behind it all. If we want a job that is also a vocation, we should not passively wait around for it to appear out of thin air. Instead we should take action and endeavour to grow it like Marie Curie. How? Simply by devoting ourselves to work that gives us deep fulfilment through meaning, flow and freedom (though a fourteen-hour day might be overdoing it a little). Over time, a tangible and inspiring goal may quietly germinate, grow larger, and eventually flower into life.

A Message from Zorba

Many people baulk at the final hurdle of making a career change. They've done months of thinking through the options, perhaps undertaken a few branching projects, tried some conversational research, and eventually realized what the best career choice would be. And then they stop, faced by a paralysing fear. Doubts start running through their head. What if I've made a terrible mistake and the job ends up a disaster rather than a source of fulfilment? Wouldn't it be safer just to hold back on handing in my notice, and wait until I'm absolutely certain that I've found the right career to move into?

This kind of anxiety is perfectly normal. There is no escape from the fact that, in the end, changing career is a risk. It is full of uncertainties and unknowns, no matter how much we prepare ourselves for it.

How can we make that final leap into the darkness?

While researching this book, I asked many people this question. And they all gave me a similar answer. Sameera Khan, who resigned from her full-time corporate law job and is now working in the social enterprise sector and as a freelance lawyer, told me what she had learned from her own experience:

> I went to an amazing career coach. I couldn't believe I was seeing a career coach, it was embarrassing to admit to friends, embarrassing to admit to myself. After a couple of sessions she said, 'Well, you know you've got to quit your job, otherwise you'll be stuck in this despair forever. Once you quit, some of the fog will be lifted. So we've got to set a date.' So we set a date of July 1 and this was in the middle of May! I said that was really soon, and she replied, 'Well, you're not going to do it otherwise.' And of course I wasn't going to. So I did quit on July 1. Ultimately, when you want to quit your job you just have to do it.

Indeed, the inconvenient truth is that there comes a point when you need to stop thinking and just do it. This is one of the most ancient pieces of wisdom for the art of living. Like the idea of having a purposeful goal in life, it has been articulated in many forms over the centuries. Its most famous expression, in Western culture, appears in the *Odes* of the Roman poet Horace: *carpe diem*, he advised, seize the day – before time runs out on you. In the Rabbinical tradition there is a saying attributed to the sage Hillel the Elder: 'And if not now, when?' The Danish philosopher Søren Kierkegaard gave us the idea of a 'leap of faith'. For a literary version try George Eliot's *Middlemarch*: 'I would not creep along the coast but steer out in mid-sea, by guidance of the stars.'

The ubiquity of this ideal reveals an adventurous spirit in humanity, one fired by a knowledge that life is preciously short, and that to make the most of it – to 'suck out all the marrow of life', as Thoreau put it – we have no choice but to take risks that promise us the gift of a more profound and vibrant existence.

There are, without doubt, ways of making that final step towards change easier. By ensuring we have some financial safety net – perhaps a few months of savings stashed away – we can allay our fear of destitution if our new job fails to work out. We can also put our faith in the power of public declarations: by openly telling friends and family that we are about to change career, we may begin to shift our own expectations and give ourselves more courage to act. And don't forget the power of the written word: try writing your own obituary. Imagine yourself in the future, looking back over your life, and write the story of what you did, or hoped you had done. It is up to you to decide whether or not, at the age of 36, you left your job in financial services to work for a local community theatre, or to become a freelancing wide achiever. Writing your obituary is a startlingly effective way to help avoid a corrosive feeling of regret that you did not take your life in new directions when you had the chance.

There is one last way to break with your past and begin a new stage of your career journey, which is to take some advice that appears at the end of the 1964 film *Zorba the Greek*.

Zorba, the great lover of life, is sitting on the beach with the repressed and bookish Basil, an Englishman who has come to a tiny Greek island with the hope of setting up a small business. The elaborate cable system that Zorba has designed and built for Basil to bring logs down the mountainside has just collapsed on its very first trial. Their whole entrepreneurial venture is in complete ruins, a failure before it has even begun. And that is the moment when Zorba unveils his philosophy of life to Basil:

> ZORBA: Damn it boss, I like you too much not to say it. You've got everything except one thing: madness! A man needs a little madness, or else . . .
>
> BASIL: Or else?
>
> ZORBA: . . . he never dares cut the rope and be free.

Basil then stands up and, completely out of character, asks Zorba to teach him how to dance. The Englishman has finally learned that life is there to be lived with passion, that risks are there to be taken, the day is there to be seized. To do otherwise is a disservice to life itself.

Zorba's words are one of the great messages for the human quest in search of the good life. Most of us live bound by our fears and inhibitions. Yet if we are to move beyond them, if we are to cut the rope and be free, we need to treat life as an experiment and discover the little bit of madness that lies within us all.

Are you ready to take that final step to be free?

Homework

If you are hungry for more ideas on the art of working, the following books, films and websites will provide the necessary sustenance. All of them, in different ways, helped to inspire the thoughts that appear in this book.

1. The Age of Fulfilment

A good starting place to explore the possibilities for a fulfilling career is Studs Terkel's extraordinary oral history *Working*, in which everyday workers, from bank tellers to barbers, talk about what their jobs mean to them. Also treat yourself to Po Bronson's *What Should I Do With My Life?*, a compilation of real-life stories describing the challenges and fears involved in changing career. *Salesman* (1968) is a riveting documentary about four door-to-door salesmen selling very expensive Bibles to low-income families in the United States. The way they deal with constant rejection, homesickness and burnout provides lessons for anyone in search of a fulfilling job.

2. A Short History of Career Confusion

On the history of work, the best overview is Richard Donkin's *Blood, Sweat and Tears: The Evolution of Work*. Theodore Zeldin's remarkable *An Intimate History of Humanity* is a history of human relationships from the earliest times and across all cultures, chronicling how the past has shaped the way we approach work and other areas of life such as love and time. *The Paradox of Choice* by psychologist Barry Schwartz provides useful insights into why we get so confused about career choice. There is a witty and wise TED talk by philosopher Alain de Botton on our inherited cultural ideas about success and failure at: www.ted.com/talks/lang/eng/alain_de_botton_a_kinder_gentler_philosophy_of_success.html. For a critique of the Myers–Briggs Type Indicator, read David Pittenger's article 'Measuring the MBTI . . . And Coming Up Short' at www.indiana.edu/~jobtalk/articles/develop/mbti.pdf.

3. Giving Meaning to Work

The temptations of a big salary are analysed in Oliver James's *Affluenza*, in which he argues that we place an excessively high value on acquiring money and possessions, and wanting to look good in the eyes of others. Oliver Stone's film *Wall Street* (1987) delves further into this theme in his parable of the 1980s corporate raider Gordon Gekko. The story of Anita Roddick's attempts to bring her ethics into the workplace appear in her autobiography *Business as Unusual*. If you are keen to cultivate your talents and experiment with being a wide achiever rather than a high achiever, get yourself a copy of Charles's Nicholl's biography *Leonardo da Vinci: The Flights of the Mind.*

4. Act First, Reflect Later

The psychology and sociology of risk are discussed in Richard Sennett's profound and beautifully written meditation on modern work, *The Corrosion of Character*. In *Working Identity*, professor of organizational behaviour Herminia Ibarra outlines principles for career reinvention, busting several myths about career change in the process. Solidly grounded in analysis of countless case studies, this is one of the finest academic books on what it takes to find fulfilling work. Out of psychologist Mihaly Csikszentmihalyi's numerous works on flow experience, the best is *Flow: The Classic Work on How to Achieve Happiness*. The film *American Beauty* (1999) examines a family whose members make some life-changing choices, including a father who gives up his career in advertising in search of a more meaningful existence. Political writer George Monbiot offers some timeless and inspiring advice on how to make career choices at www.monbiot.com/archives/2000/06/09/choose-life/.

5. The Longing for Freedom

Colin Ward's *Anarchy in Action* is the ultimate handbook for those in search of greater freedom in their working lives. *Screw Work, Let's Play* by John Williams offers useful practical tips on how to make it in the freelance world. One of the best ways to wean yourself off the work ethic is by reading Bertrand Russell's essay *In Praise of Idleness.* In *Walden,* the nineteenth-century naturalist Henry David Thoreau offers a compelling and poetic vision of simple living, while a programme for turning it into reality can be found in *Your Money or Your Life* by Joe Dominguez and Vicki Robin. Illuminating on women's role as workers are Rosalind Miles's scintillating *The Women's History of the World* and Simone de Beauvoir's feminist blockbuster *The Second Sex.* The tensions between career aspirations and family life are exposed in the tear-inducing film *Kramer vs. Kramer* (1979).

6. How to Grow a Vocation

Follow the career story and scientific discoveries of Marie Curie in *Madame Curie,* the biography by her daughter Eve Curie. Join the immortal Alexis Zorba (Anthony Quinn) and the staid Englishman Basil (Alan Bates) on an isolated Greek Island in the film *Zorba the Greek* (1964). Zorba teaches Basil about the art of taking risks and going in new directions in working life, and delivers his famous line: 'A man needs a little madness, or else he never dares cut the rope and be free.' In my book *The Wonderbox: Curious Histories of How to Live,* I reveal what history can teach us about finding a job we love and becoming more adventurous in the way we make decisions about our careers and other realms of everyday life.

A comprehensive bibliography is available online at: www.panmacmillan.com/theschooloflife

Notes

1. The Age of Fulfilment

1 Thomas, Keith, *The Ends of Life: Roads to Fulfilment in Early Modern England*, Oxford: Oxford University Press, 2009, p.8.

2 www.opp.eu.com/SiteCollectionDocuments/pdfs/dream-research.pdf; http://news.bbc.co.uk/1/hi/world/americas/8440630.stm

3 www.statistics.gov.uk/articles/labour_market_trends/jobmobility_nov03.pdf , p.543.

4 Svendsen, Lars, *Work*, Stocksfield: Acumen, 2008, p.5.

5 Batchelor, Stephen, *Buddhism Without Beliefs: A Contemporary Guide to Awakening*, London: Bloomsbury, 1998, p.25.

6 Burckhardt, Jacob, *The Civilization of the Renaissance in Italy*, Oxford and London: Phaidon, 1945, p.81; Greenblatt, Stephen, *Renaissance Self-Fashioning: From More to Shakespeare*, Chicago: University of Chicago Press, 2005, p.2; Krznaric, Roman, *The First Beautiful Game: Stories of Obsession in Real Tennis*, Oxford: Ronaldson Publications, 2006, chapter 11.

2. A Short History of Career Confusion

7 www.careerplanner.com/ListOfCareers.cfm.

8 Franklin, Benjamin, *Autobiography and Other Writings*, Oxford: Oxford University Press, 1998, pp.9–14.

9 Marx, Karl, *The Marxist Reader*, ed. Emile Burns, New York: Avenel Books, 1982, pp.273–274.

10 Miles, Rosalind, *The Women's History of the World*, London: Paladin, 1989, p.191.

11 Hobsbawm, Eric, *The Age of Revolution 1789–1848*, New York: Vintage, 1996, pp.189–194.
12 www.bls.gov/mlr/1999/12/art1full.pdf; www.voxeu.org/index/php?q=node/3946.
13 Miles, Rosalind, *The Women's History of the World*, p.271.
14 Schwartz, Barry, *The Paradox of Choice: Why Less Is More*, New York: Harper Perennial, 2005, pp.2, 9–10, 221.
15 Ibid. pp.9–10, 24–25; http://www.ted.com/talks/barry_schwartz_on_the_paradox_of_choice.html.
16 Ibid. pp.118–119, 140–141.
17 Ibid. pp.221–227.
18 www.cambridgeassessment.org.uk.
19 world-countries.net/archives/2218.
20 Schwartz, Barry, *The Paradox of Choice: Why Less Is More*, pp. 72–73.
21 Ibid. 149–150.
22 Pope, Mark, 'A Brief History of Career Counselling in the United States', *The Career Development Quarterly*, Vol.48, No.3, 2000, p.196.
23 Parsons, Frank, *Choosing a Vocation*, Boston, Houghton Mifflin, 1909, pp.21–22, 27–31.
24 Ibid. pp.133–136.
25 Hershenson, David B., 'A Head of Its Time: Career Counselling's Roots in Phrenology', *Career Development Quarterly*, Vol.57, No.2, 2008, pp.181–190; Lindqvist, Sven, *The Skull Measurer's Mistake*, New York: New Press, 1997; www.archive.org/stream/systemofphrenolooocombuoft#page/n7/mode/2up.
26 Bjork, Robert A. and Daniel Druckman, *In the Mind's Eye: Enhancing Human Performance*, Washington: National Academies Press, 1991, pp.99–100; Gregory, Robert J., *Psychological Testing: History, Principles, Applications*, 4th edn, Boston: Pearson, p.524; Hunsley, John, Catherine M. Lee and James M. Wood, 'Controversial and Questionable Assessment Techniques' in Scott O. Lilienfield, Steven Jay Lynn and Jeffrey M. Lohr (eds), *Science and Pseudoscience in Clinical Psychology*, New York: The Guilford Press, 2003, pp.61–64; Boyle, Gregory, 'Myers–Briggs Type Indicator (MBTI): Some Psychometric Limitations', Bond University Humanities and Social Sciences Papers, No.26, 1995; McCrae, Robert and Paul Costa Jr, 'Reinterpreting the Myers–Briggs Type Indicator From

the Perspective of the Five-Factor Model of Personality', *Journal of Personality*, Vol.57, No.1, 1989, pp.17–40.

27 Pittenger, David, 'Cautionary Comments Regarding the Myers–Briggs Type Indicator', *Consulting Psychology Journal: Practice and Research*, Vol.57, No.3, 2005, p.214.

28 Ibid; Boyle, Gregory, 'Myers–Briggs Type Indicator (MBTI): Some Psychometric Limitations', Bond University Humanities and Social Sciences Papers, No.26.

29 Hunsley, John, Catherine M. Lee and James M. Wood, 'Controversial and Questionable Assessment Techniques' in Scott O. Lilienfield, Steven Jay Lynn and Jeffrey M. Lohr (eds), *Science and Pseudoscience in Clinical Psychology*, p.62; McCrae, Robert and Paul Costa Jr, 'Reinterpreting the Myers–Briggs Type Indicator From the Perspective of the Five-Factor Model of Personality', *Journal of Personality*, Vol.57, No.1, 1989, p.20.

30 OPP Unlocking Potential, *MBTI Step 1 Question Book*, European English edn, Oxford: OPP, 1998, p.1; OPP Unlocking Potential, *Introduction to Type and Careers*, European English edn, Oxford: OPP, 2000, p.26.

31 Pittenger, David, 'Measuring the MBTI ... And Coming Up Short', *Journal of Career Planning and Placement*, Vol.54, pp.48–53; Pittenger, David, 'Cautionary Comments Regarding the Myers–Briggs Type Indicator', *Consulting Psychology Journal: Practice and Research*, Vol.57, No.3, pp. 211, 217; personal communication with David Pittenger, 5/9/11. See also Hunsley, John, Catherine M. Lee and James M. Wood, 'Controversial and Questionable Assessment Techniques' in Scott O. Lilienfield, Steven Jay Lynn and Jeffrey M. Lohr (eds), *Science and Pseudoscience in Clinical Psychology*, p.63; Bjork, Robert A. and Daniel Druckman, *In the Mind's Eye: Enhancing Human Performance*, pp.99–101.

32 Ibarra, Herminia, *Working Identity: Unconventional Strategies for Reinventing Your Career*, Boston: Harvard Business School Press, 2004, pp.35–37.

3. Giving Meaning to Work

33 Argyle, Michael, *The Social Psychology of Work*, London: Penguin, 1989, pp. 99–101.

34 Layard, Richard, *Happiness: Lessons from a New Science*, London: Allen Lane, 2005, pp.32–33; for more recent research, see www.pnas.org/content/107/38/16489.full.pdf+html?sid=aac48a0b-d009-4ce6-8c14-7f97c5310e15.
35 Seligman, Martin, *Authentic Happiness: Using the New Positive Psychology to Realize Your Potential for Lasting Fulfillment*, Nicholas Brealey, 2002, p.49; James, Oliver, *Affluenza: How to be Successful and Stay Sane*, London: Vermilion, 2007, p.52.
36 Gerhardt, Sue, *The Selfish Society: How We All Forgot to Love One Another and Made Money Instead*, London: Simon & Schuster, 2010, pp.32–33.
37 www.guardian.co.uk/money/2011/jul/15/happiness-work-why-counts; www.theworkfoundation.com/assets/docs/publications/162_newwork_goodwork.pdf.
38 Schwartz, Barry, *The Paradox of Choice: Why Less Is More*, p.190.
39 Rousseau, Jean-Jacques, *A Discourse Upon The Origin And The Foundation Of The Inequality Among Mankind*, 1754, http://www.gutenberg.org/files/11136/11136.txt.
40 Lewis, Clive Staples, 'The Inner Ring', 1944, www.lewissociety.org/innerring.php.
41 Sennett, Richard, *The Corrosion of Character: The Personal Consequences of Work in the New Capitalism*, New York: Norton, 2003, p.3.
42 Arendt, Hannah, *The Human Condition*, Chicago: University of Chicago Press, 1989, p.18–19; Csikszentmihalyi, Mihaly, *Flow: The Classic Work on How to Achieve Happiness*, London: Rider, 2002, p.218.
43 Gardner, Howard, Mihaly Csikszentmihalyi and William Damon, *Good Work: When Excellence and Ethics Meet*, New York: Basic Books, 2001, pp.ix, 5.
44 Singer, Peter, *How Are We To Live? Ethics in an Age of Self-interest*, Oxford: Oxford University Press, 1997, pp.255–258.
45 Roddick, Anita, *Business As Unusual: My Entrepreneurial Journey, Profits With Principles*, Chichester: Anita Roddick Books, 2005, p.37.
46 Ibid. pp.83, 96, 122, 157, 179, 205.
47 www.satyamag.com/jan05/roddick.html.
48 Roddick, Anita, *Business As Unusual: My Entrepreneurial Journey, Profits With Principles*, pp.18, 92, 246.
49 Krznaric, Roman, *The First Beautiful Game: Stories of Obsession in Real Tennis*, pp.72–84.

50 Quoted in Williams, John, *Screw Work, Let's Play: How to do what you love and get paid for it*, Harlow: Prentice Hall, 2010, p.3.
51 Saul, John Ralston, *Voltaire's Bastards: The Dictatorship of Reason in the West*, London: Sinclair Stevenson, 1992, p.474; Zeldin, Theodore, *An Intimate History of Humanity*, London: Minerva, 1995, pp.197–198.
52 Csikszentmihalyi, Mihaly, *Flow: The Classic Work on How to Achieve Happiness*, p.155.
53 Ibarra, Herminia, *Working Identity: Unconventional Strategies for Reinventing Your Career*, p.xi.
54 Quoted in Nicholl, Charles, *Leonardo da Vinci: The Flights of the Mind*, London: Penguin, 2005, p.7.
55 Cameron, Julia, *The Artist's Way: A Course in Discovering and Recovering Your Creative Self*, London: Pan, 1995, p.39; Williams, John, *Screw Work, Let's Play: How to do what you love and get paid for it*, p.37.

4. *Act First, Reflect Later*

56 www.opp.eu.com/SiteCollectionDocuments/pdfs/dream-research.pdf.
57 Quoted in Sennett, Richard, *The Corrosion of Character: The Personal Consequences of Work in the New Capitalism*, p.82.
58 Seligman, Martin, *Authentic Happiness: Using the New Positive Psychology to Realize Your Potential for Lasting Fulfilment*, pp.30–31; Csikszentmihalyi, Mihaly, *Flow: The Classic Work on How to Achieve Happiness*, p.169. Special thanks to Rob Archer for helping me think about this issue.
59 Ibarra, Herminia, *Working Identity: Unconventional Strategies for Reinventing Your Career*, pp.xii, 16, 18, 91.
60 Ibid. p.45.
61 Ibid. p.113–120.
62 Csikszentmihalyi, Mihaly, *Beyond Boredom and Anxiety: Experiencing Flow in Work and Play*, San Francisco: Jossey-Bass, 2000, pp.35–36, 132, 137; Csikszentmihalyi, Mihaly, *Flow: The Classic Work on How to Achieve Happiness*, p.4.
63 Ibid. pp.48–67.
64 Ibid. p.152.

5. *The Longing for Freedom*

65 Schumacher, E.F., *Good Work*, London: Abacus, 1980, p.50.
66 www.theworkfoundation.com/assets/docs/publications/162_newwork_goodwork.pdf, p.29.
67 Fromm, Erich, *Fear of Freedom*, London: Routledge, 1960, pp.19–20, 85.
68 Ward, Colin, *Anarchism: A Very Short Introduction*, Oxford: Oxford University Press, 2004, p.49; www.guardian.co.uk/money/2011/jul/15/happiness-work-why-counts.
69 Ward, Colin, *Anarchy in Action*, London: Freedom Press, 1996, pp.94–5.
70 www.fsb.org.uk/policy/images/2011%2004%20self%20employment%20one%20page%20briefing.pdf; www.theworkfoundation.com/assets/docs/publications/145_Joy_of_Work.pdf, p.14.
71 Quoted in, Williams, John, *Screw Work, Let's Play: How to do what you love and get paid for it*, p.1.
72 http://www.thedailybeast.com/newsweek/2008/05/21/my-ebay-job.html.
73 Krakauer, Jon, *Into the Wild*, London: Pan Books, 2007.
74 www.guardian.co.uk/money/2000/oct/01/workandcareers.madeleinebunting2.
75 Robinson, Bryan, *Chained to the Desk: A Guidebook for Workaholics, Their Partners and Children, and the Clinicians Who Treat Them*, New York: New York University Press, 2001.
76 Russell, Bertrand, *In Praise of Idleness and Other Essays*, London: Unwin, 1976.
77 www.workfoundation.com/assets/docs/publications/177_About%20time%20for%20change.pdf, p.5–6.
78 Lerner, Steve, *Eco-Pioneers: Practical Visionaries Solving Today's Environmental Problems*, Boston: MIT Press, 1998, pp.71–72; Dominguez, Joe and Vicki Robin, *Your Money or Your Life: Transforming Your Relationship with Money and Achieving Financial Independence*, New York: Penguin, 1999.
79 De Beauvoir, Simone, *The Second Sex*, Harmondsworth: Penguin, 1972, pp.689–690, 703.
80 Nicolson, Paula, *Having It All? Choices for Today's Superwoman*, Chichester: John Wiley, 2002, pp.19, 155.

81 www.stayathomedads.co.uk/news.html
82 www.guardian.co.uk/money/2011/jul/19-norway-dads-paternity-leave-chemin
83 Quoted in Nicolson, Paula, *Having It All? Choices for Today's Superwoman* Nicolson, pp.12–13.
84 Ibid. pp.140, 142.
85 Folbre, Nancy, *Who Pays for the Kids? Gender and the Structures of Constraint*, London: Routledge, 1994, pp.2–3; http://www.legalandgeneralgroup.com/media-centre/press-releases/2011/group-news-release-876.html; www.sociology.leeds.ac.uk/assets/files/research/circle/valuing-carers.pdf.

6. *How to Grow a Vocation*

86 Quoted in Thomas, Keith, *The Ends of Life: Roads to Fulfilment in Early Modern England*, p.vii.
87 Quoted in Meilaender, Gilbert C., *Working: Its Meaning and Its Limits*, Notre Dame: University of Notre Dame Press, 2000, p.107.
88 Frankl, Victor, *Man's Search for Meaning: An Introduction to Logotherapy*, London: Hodder and Stoughton, 1987, pp.107, 110.
89 Csikszentmihalyi, Mihaly, *Flow: The Classic Work on How to Achieve Happiness*, pp.217–218.
90 Curie, Eve, *Madam Curie*, London: William Heinemann, 1938, p.134.
91 Ibid. p.113.
92 Ibid. pp.150–151, 162–163.
93 Bronson, Po, *What Should I Do With My Life: The True Story of People Who Answered the Ultimate Question*, London: Vintage, 2004, pp.291–292.

Acknowledgements

It has been a great pleasure working with Alain de Botton, the series editor, who has provided excellent ideas and advice throughout the course of creating this book. Thanks to Liz Gough, Dusty Miller, Tania Adams, Katie James, Kate Hewson and everyone at Pan Macmillan for all their backing and encouragement. My agent, Margaret Hanbury, has been tremendously supportive as always, offering wise counsel and inventive thoughts, as has Henry de Rougemont at the Hanbury Agency.

The origins of my interest in work go back to my years working with the historian and thinker Theodore Zeldin at The Oxford Muse, which gave me the opportunity to talk to people from every walk of life about their struggles to find a fulfilling career, from warehouse workers to CEOs, from pole dancers to Buddhist monks. I was later inspired by my involvement with The School of Life, where I teach and helped design the courses on work. Thanks to everyone there, including Morgwn Rimel, Caroline Brimmer, Harriet Warden and Mark Brickman, and to Sophie Howarth, the founding director. My ideas have also benefited from conversations with friends in the Relational Politics group in Oxford: Sue Gerhardt, Adam Swift, Jean Knox, Sarah Stewart-Brown and Sue Weaver. Thanks too to David Pittenger at Marshall University.

I could not have written this book without people from many countries generously sharing their career stories with me. I learned a huge amount from their experiences and insights. They include: Amanda Beckles, Andy Bell, Andy Kwok, Annalise Moser, Anne Marie Graham, Brian Campbell, Cathy O'Neil, Chris Dean, Clare Taylor, Esther Freeman, Fiona Robyn, Fiona Sanson, Flutra Qatja, George Marshall, Helena Fosh, Iain King, James Attlee, Jonty Olliff-Cooper, Karen Byrne, Karen Macmillan, Keira O'Mara, Kirsten Puls, Laura van Bouchout, Lee Rotbart, Lisa Brideau, Lisa Gormley, Meike Brunkhorst, Paula Ligo, Rob Archer, Rupert Denyer, Sam Lewis, Sameera Khan, Sarah Best, Sharon Harvey, Tom Burrough, Trevor Dean, Wayne Davies and Yvonne Braeunlich. Please note that I have changed the names of some people I quote in the text.

Special thanks to my parents, Anna and Peter Krznaric, for all their support while completing this book, to my children Casimir and Siri for tolerating my long absences, and to Kate Raworth for more than I can say.

I dedicate this book to another book, which has done so much to shape how I think about work: Studs Terkel's superb oral history *Working: People Talk About What They Do All Day and How They Feel About What They Do.*

Picture and Text Acknowledgements

Every effort has been made to contact the copyright holders of the material reproduced in this book. If any have been inadvertently overlooked the publisher will be pleased to make restitution at the earliest opportunity.

Page 44 extract is taken from *The Selfish Society*, Sue Gerhardt (Simon & Schuster/RCW Literary Agency, 2010); Page 95 extract is taken from *Good Work*, E.F. Schumacher (Jonathan Cape, 1979) and reproduced courtesy of the Estate of E.F. Schumacher; Page 98 extract is taken from *Anarchy in Action*, Colin Ward (Freedom Press, 1973); Page 106 extract is taken from 'In Praise of Idleness', *In Praise of Idleness and other Essays* (Allen and Unwin, 1935)

The author and publisher would like to thank the following for permission to reproduce the images used in this book:

Page 11 Aerial silks artist © Thomas Barwick / Getty Images; Page 21 Girl at a spinning machine © Corbis; Page 32 Phrenology cartoon © Heritage Images / Corbis; Page 53 Anita Roddick © The Roddick Foundation; Page 61 *Vitruvian Man*, Leonardo da Vinci. Photograph © Garry Gay / Getty Images; Page 89 Jackson Pollock at work © Time & Life Pictures / Getty Images; Page 107 Bertrand Russell © Mary Evans Picture Library / Marx Memorial Library; Page 123 *The Captive Slave*, Michelangelo. Photograph © Time & Life Pictures / Getty Images; Page 133 Marie Curie © Time & Life Pictures / Getty Images; Page 138 Zorba the Greek © Moviestore Collection Ltd / Alamy.

All other images provided courtesy of the author.

Notes

If you enjoyed this book and want to read more about life's big issues, you can find out about the series, buy books and get access to exclusive content at www.panmacmillan.com/theschooloflife

If you'd like to explore ideas for everyday living, THE SCHOOL OF LIFE runs a regular programme of classes, weekends, secular sermons and events in London and other cities around the world. Browse our shop and visit www.theschooloflife.com

How to Thrive in the Digital Age
Tom Chatfield

How to Think More about Sex
Alain de Botton

How to Change the World
John-Paul Flintoff

How to Worry Less about Money
John Armstrong

How to Stay Sane
Philippa Perry

How to Find Fulfilling Work
Roman Krznaric

THESCHOOLOFLIFE.COM
TWITTER.COM/SCHOOLOFLIFE

panmacmillan.com
twitter.com/panmacmillan